"The thing that drives a real pro
is simply inner satisfaction. That's all."

*Merlin Olsen*

"A great part of art consists in imitation.
For the whole conduct of life is based on this:

what we admire in others
we want to do ourselves."

—*Quintilian*

# The Winner's Edge

## What The All-Pros Say About Success

### by Bob Oates, Jr.

Mayflower Books
New York, New York

Produced for publication by
Christopher, Maclay, and Co.

Produced for publication by Christopher,
Maclay, and Co.
P.O. Box 481-B, Fairfield, Iowa
Library of Congress Card Catalogue Number
80-82519

Printed in the United States of America

The Winner's Edge™ and the Triangle of
Success™ are trade marks and service marks of
Christopher, Maclay, and Co.

ISBN: 0 - 8317-9455 - 0

Designed by David Johnston
Production art by David Bousfield and Mary Murphy

# Dedication

This book is for my parents,
whose love has been the basis of my life.

# The Line-up

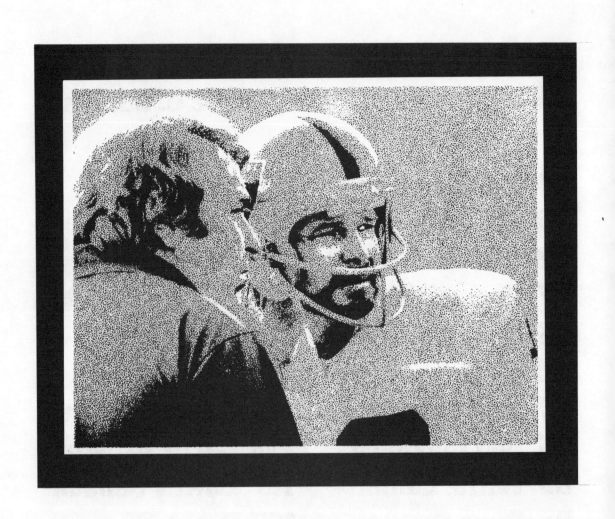

# Author's Foreword

In the last ten years I've had the chance to talk with some of the best football players who ever played the game. It's been a privilege. I've enjoyed it.

And looking back at the written interviews, the words-on-paper record of those personal encounters, I have been struck anew with the vibrant and meaningful things these people have to say.

All-Pro football players have succeeded in an intensely challenging profession. They have been force-fed some lessons that can help us all.

Football is only a game, of course, just a weekend diversion that some lucky men get to play well out of childhood. But, game or no, once a man steps onto that white-lined field, he submits himself to a demanding test. Pro football is a confrontation of muscle and guile, a physical battle that is computer complex. No other sport comes close to matching this extreme mix of brawn and brains; none demands such a wide range of human capabilities, from brute strength to fingertip skill, from raw courage to chess-level creativity.

This is why no one sneaks up on lasting success in the pro game. Even the most talented of the athletes must learn to tap the fullness of their potential and unlock the power of their focused will. Everyone on a pro football field is living full-out.

And this is why we love to watch them play their game. It is thrilling to see people perform feats of great artistry, daring and desire. A quarterback who stands solid, reading the defense like a computer print-out despite the storm-wild battle raging around him, not only demonstrates great athletic skill with his precision passes. He also demonstrates his mastery of fear and his power of profound concentration. A running back who scrabbles for the last yard every time is not just a man playing a game. He is a living expression of human drive and determination.

This is not a world for people who settle. It is not a life for those who won't seek out the best that is in them. No one reaches the top of his profession—that exclusive circle of repeated All-Pros—who is not, in many ways at least, a truly remarkable human being.

Hero worship is not easy at this stage in our history, of course. We have seen too many idols fall, too many leaders go to seed—or to jail. All-American perfection is beyond our expectation. Frank Merriwell doesn't live here any more.

Yet it still seems right to recognize excellence where it can be found. We don't need to consider our leading statesmen and scientists—and athletes—perfect in order to learn from them the best that they know. By putting our attention on the strengths of these men, we can bring those strengths into our lives. For it is a truth of the human mechanism: what we put our attention on grows in us.

It's not that these athletes force their ideas on others. They don't see themselves as exceptionally wise. They aren't, most of them, artists or mathematicians or lawyers, though some of them graduate to these levels. What they are is football players, and their truths emerge naturally when you talk to them about their sport.

In the bulk of these discussions, confronted with one lively personality or another, I simply let the conversations range where they would, following each player down the path that excited him most. But these are the modern gladiators, warriors of mind and body, and the rigorous lessons of their lives come out spontaneously. Even when the talk is all football, the message of the man emerges in style and tone—in the mental and emotional approach that is taken. Frequently, moreover, the discussions grow more thoughtful and abstract, and the gut-real lessons of the game are extended into the rest of life. Techniques of concentration come out, secrets of confidence and motivation, lessons on preparedness.

Of all the points brought up in this way, one theme tends to dominate. Even in a world of 250-pound people, immense men who, when seen moving in a group through an airport, say, can seem to be representatives of another species, even in this world where intense physical combat is a weekly reality, the emphasis of repeated winners is on the immaterial, intangible guide that is the human mind. Their game may seem at first but a crashing contest for the plastic-protected body, but most of the All-Pros say the real battle is mental, a confrontation in consciousness.

Furthermore, many of these athletes take specific action to "beef up" their minds. They train their intellects just as they train their bodies. Several of the interviews give specific recipes for increasing confidence, improving concentration, programming mental success and maintaining control in a crisis.

And the ideas of these men cover much more ground, from finding the dead spot in a zone defense to updating the mechanics of American democracy. These are people who know how to succeed in a world of intense challenge. Nearly everything they say, at least to my ear, can be put to good use by those who seek growth. The subject is football, the examples are football, but the lessons are as large as life.

It is a pleasure to bring this book out, and those of us who have worked on it have tried to make it worthy of the athletes and their sport.

One of our interests has been the creation of the handworked photo-art of each athlete. For the work on this art, I would like to thank the original photographers, as well as my good old friends David Johnston and Jim Chaffin. And while I'm giving out thanks, I would also like to express my appreciation to David Boss and to National

Football League Properties for the opportunity to write some of the interviews in the first place, and the right to re-print them here; to Joe Namath, Jimmy Walsh, and Little, Brown, and Company, for permission to extract material from the book Joe and I did several years ago, *A Matter of Style*; to the Los Angeles Times for permission to reprint my father's interview with Merlin Olsen; to John Olson at Kachina Typesetting in Tempe, Arizona for fast, accurate and beautiful type; to R. R. Donnelley, the excellent printers headquartered in Chicago; to Bob Cobb at Cobb/Dunlop Publishing Services in New York, a magician for generating finished books; to Tim Waterstone, Jim Mann and the wonderful new family at Mayflower Books, the distributing publisher of this book; and to Monte Guild, who made the project possible. And finally, as a proper conclusion, I wish to express my gratitude and devotion to my wife, Patricia Ferguson Oates, whose grace has made my life whole, who lives at the heart of my every thought and act.

**Bob Oates, Jr.**
**Fairfield, Iowa**

# Introduction: The Triangle Of Success

## By Christopher Attwood

*Author's note: Herewith a few bonus pages in a book that is basically football. People who have picked up this volume simply because they love the game and the people who play it can skip this brief section with no loss to their enjoyment. But for people who have more than a casual interest in the basic principles which lead to excellence and success in any field, I am happy to be able to present the following essay.*

*It was only a few months ago that I first had the chance to talk with Christopher Attwood about a set of ideas he calls the Triangle of Success. Attwood is a management consultant who owns and operates his own firm, and when I first heard the exposition of his Triangle, I could see why people go to him for advice. His ideas are both simple and powerful, a most compelling combination. As soon as I heard his talk I decided to ask him if he would collaborate on an introduction. I hope others find it as illuminating and entertaining—and as relevant to the football experience—as I have. (In the back of the book, by way of summary, I have gathered some of the athletes' more incisive quotes and grouped them under the headings suggested by Attwood's Triangle.)*

When you walk into the offices of Attwood Management Consultants the first thing you see is a carefully positioned poster. You can't miss it. Across the top the poster announces itself in a bold headline: "The Triangle of Success." Underneath, in three-pointed format with the first phrase at the top, it says, "Strong Thought—Dynamic Action—Honest Assessment" (see figure at right).

What is the Triangle of Success exactly? Why does a management consultant firm put it up on the wall? There is no better place than a football book to answer those questions. In fact, I believe the Triangle of Success and *The Winner's Edge* have a great deal in common. I can show you what I mean most easily with a brief description of the Triangle, putting all the examples in terms of football. Here, then, with a few classic quotes included, is a football definition of the Triangle of Success.

## Strong Thought

*"Thoughts rule the world."*—Emerson

Thought is the basis of action. Action is the basis of achievement. The achievement of success is based on the power of the mind.

Football players learn this lesson or they don't last. First they must set the strong mental goal of winning a position—and then winning games—or they don't have the strength to cut through the football flak. First, as the coaches say, they

# The Triangle Of Success

## Strong Thought

## Dynamic Action

## Honest Assessment

must have *desire*. They must have the right mental attitude. They have to "want it".

Second, players must master the intricate mental challenges of the sport. They must understand the game in all its nuances, or be suckered and fooled repeatedly. The weekly game plan is based on exhaustive film research and close use of computer readouts. Players must know the plan in every detail, and remember it in the midst of Sunday's pressure.

Even in a game as physical as football, victory is based in the mind—as so many of the athletes in this book point out.

## Dynamic Action

"With slight efforts how could one obtain great results?"—Euripides

Thought is sterile without action. Action makes thoughts real. And action, to accomplish, must be forceful, intense, and dynamic.

A football player, once he has "programmed" his mind correctly, must go out on the field and make it happen. He has to "go for it". He needs perseverance under pressure. There has to be an all-out effort on every play for sixty minutes. As Joe Namath said, "First you study up. Then you turn yourself loose."

There is no room for half efforts. The tentative are demolished by big men who know what they want and won't stand not to get it. In the coaching cliché, "Even if you are going to make a mistake, make it full speed." Only dynamic action can bring victory. Lloyd George put it this way almost a century ago: "You can't cross a chasm in two small jumps."

## Honest Assessment

"The superior man will watch over himself."
—Confucius

Strong thought leads to strong action. But is the action on course? Are we going where we headed? A successful person has to be a self-correcting rocket, continually refining his course.

Football people know this better than most. It's true that while they play, the athletes throw themselves headlong into action. If a player tries to examine his form while his opponents are bearing down on him, he will freeze and be trampled. Action must be full-bore, all-consuming.

But when play ceases, Honest Assessment takes over. During a game there is continuous consultation with the coaches on the bench and in the press box. Every sideline conference is a group analysis of events. Then, most definitively, there is film day, when the movies of last week's game are studied with microscopic, unrelenting intensity. Every move by every man is noted and graded. Mistakes can be eliminated. Success is reinforced. And rapid progress toward group goals is reasserted. It is a simple and practical example of the dictum of Socrates, "The unexamined life is not worth living."

So that's the Triangle of Success, football style. And I must say that football style is one of the most effective ways we have found to introduce this concept to any new group. As you will learn in this book—among many other things, I'm sure—pro football players *live* the truth of the Triangle. When they talk about their experiences, moreover, you can *feel* it. Abstract ideas become gut-real experience. They communicate.

And, it goes without saying, I'm glad they make these points so clear. It's always amazing to me, for instance, how many people don't know it would help to sit down and *think* every day. Just five minutes, ten minutes, a little space to write down goals, figure out the daily game plan. It's the same for activity. It's so easy to let time slip away without noticing it go. A little excess chatter, a little too long at lunch, an afternoon gone to fatigue—Dynamic Action is a rare art. And as for regular self-assessment, few people have ever even given it a thought. People usually just function until they fall asleep, get up the next day and plunge in again. Regular monitoring of aims and efficiency is, in most circles, a non-concept.

Take it all together, the players in this book can do us quite a favor. They can bring some simple truths to light that promise to help us a great deal.

I don't mean to say the Triangle of Success covers all the points made by all twenty of these men. Far from it. In fact, the most exciting and impressive thing about these interviews, to me at least, is precisely their diversity: twenty strong personalities with twenty different slants on how to succeed in a terribly demanding sport.

But I do mean to recommend the Triangle as a starting point for meeting these All-Pros. I don't think you'll find any of these people who does not, in his own way, expand upon at least one of the three points—Strong Thought, Dynamic Action and Honest Assessment. And I think the Triangle can help make sense of the different ideas. It helps to have three big boxes to file things in.

There is one final point I wish to make. It's an idea we always emphasize at Attwood Management. It's the kind of point that Joe Greene, Willie Lanier, Dewey Selmon and others make so well in this book. It's a thought usually placed under the label *character*.

It is simply this: We DO something to BE somebody.

The point to accomplishment is to become someone accomplished. This does not mean, for football players, say, that winning the Super Bowl is what makes them great. The point is just the reverse. In many ways at least, you have to get great in order to win the Super Bowl. We have to make something of our SELVES in order to MAKE something of ourselves. It is a question of character, of our inner make-up, of our skills and courage and dedication and heart. We must develop these inner qualities to become a winner. Seeking excellence makes us excellent.

And if we grow—if our thought becomes stronger, our activity more dynamic, our assessment more honest—this new "us" is ours to keep. It continues past whatever contest called it forth. Win or lose, it can't be taken away from us. This is what Cervantes meant when he said, "Every man is the son of his own works." The best effect of the search for success is that it makes us re-create ourselves.

This is undoubtedly why O. J. Simpson was so moved by a quote from Horace Greeley. Simpson had paid his dues. He had reached the pinnacle of success in every normal sense of the word. So when he first heard this quote he jumped up and wrote it down, and then talked about it for months. It is a brief quote, and to the point. Greeley said:

**Fame is a vapor, popularity an accident, riches take wings. Only one thing endures, and that is character.**

# O.J. Simpson

"A man of character knows his
limitations—but doesn't accept them."

# O.J. Simpson

**"One of the strongest characteristics of genius is the power of lighting its own fire."**

—*John Foster*

O. J. Simpson makes you glad to be alive. On the football field he was more than a great player. He was a testimony to the genius and joy that is possible for human beings. Off the field he was, and is, a sudden success you still want to know. He went from the ghetto to glory while retaining his perspective and his shining good humor.

It was hard to get hold of him during a game, and it is hard to pin him down with words. A recitation of his NFL records provides one angle: he has the magic number, 2003, for one season; he has the season record for hundred-yard games, 11; the consecutive-game mark for hundred-yard games, 7; the season and career marks for two-hundred-yard games, 3 and 6; and the season record for touchdowns, 23.

O. J. retired after the 1979 season and headed off to the film world full-time. Some people thought his acting career would end when his football headlines did, but Simpson is several steps ahead of that already. He is doing his own film producing, and his first two TV films earned socko Nielsen ratings. O. J. Simpson is one ex-athlete who won't fade away.

This interview was conducted in 1973, just before O. J. burst out with his 2003-yard season. Though I've talked to him recently, I decided to stay with this early interview because it shows, dramatically, his before-the-fact confidence. Simpson covers a lot of ground here—from master tips on how to break the long one, through a paean to the fun of football, and on to a personal definition of the meaning of character. And along the way, as it happens, he gives some credence to Christopher Attwood's Triangle of Success, to the triad of Strong Thought, Dynamic Action and Honest Assessment (see introduction). First, his conversation bubbles over at all points with infectious, effervescent evidence of strong, confident thought. Second, when talking about his running he describes a type of action so thoroughly dynamic that he calls it "insane"—spontaneous action beyond any conscious control. And third, he extols what might be called "assessment-by-teammate"—the use of a team's collective consciousness to improve individual performance.

The interview starts, however, with Simpson's major theme of the early 1970s. It wasn't a complicated idea at all.

"Give me the ball," he said.

*You like to carry a lot?*

"The more the better. Ever since I got here to Buffalo that's all I've been saying. If I get it enough, I'll do something with it. I'll get it in there some way. My first couple of years with the Bills I didn't get the ball but two or three times a quarter—

# "There are usually one or two guys around who can carry a team. I believe I can."

usually on third and short. I know we didn't have that good a line then, but I don't care. All my blockers don't have to be the best in the business. If they're just consistent—if they make their blocks most of the time or miss them most of the time—I'll adjust to it. Just give me the ball."

*Do you think a team can do well emphasizing one man on offense?*

"I don't want to sound like I'm carrying a big head, but there are usually one or two guys around who can carry a team, who set the tone for a whole football game. Jim Brown used to be like that. Joe Namath is like that. I used to do it in college. And I believe I can do it up here, too. I think with Lou Saban coaching us now, I'm going to prove it."

*He was there last year. Didn't you feel like you did it then?*

"Not like I can. We've got an offensive line now, you know. I looked at our line in training camp last season—guys like Irv Goode who came from another team, and young guys like Reggie McKenzie and Donnie Green—and I took a look at Saban's playbook and I told everybody if I didn't gain 1,500 yards I would have a bad year."

*You only got 1,251.*

"The whole line got hurt. Everybody. But look out this year. Saban is a run-oriented coach. He's the coach I've needed for four years."

*Aren't you afraid if you carry the ball a lot you are going to get hurt?*

"I think if a runner gets hurt it's his own fault. I've only been hurt once—a twisted knee—and that was my own carelessness. I caught a kickoff near a sideline and my blockers didn't adjust over to help me. I got so mad at them I stopped concentrating on what I was doing. Somebody got a hold of me and I just stood up there and let some of the people hit me."

*Other than that you haven't been hurt?*

"Not badly. Of course, I've spent some time getting out of bounds in a hurry. The way our team was in those early years, there wasn't a whole lot of getting upfield anyway. I was trying to stay healthy and wait for things to get better."

# "I'm not thinking about anything at all. Thinking gets you caught from behind."

*What kind of ball carrier is that, stepping out instead of cracking into people?*

"You sound like some newspapermen I know. I've heard a lot about how I stutter-step up at the line, how I slow up and look around instead of blasting into the hole. But I've never been the type of runner who goes looking for people to hit. I was down at the Pro Bowl this year and Mercury Morris was there. We did some talking and we decided that we're the artist types. We like to move around and be smooth about things rather than go slamming up into holes that don't exist. I'm an optimistic type. I always believe there's a hole there somewhere if I can just find it."

*And that helps you to keep from taking unnecessary punishment?*

"Yeah, and it saves my blockers, too. I know if I'd gone charging up into my assigned hole all the time, there'd be a lot of blockers with cleat marks all up their backs. But why should I do that? Why head into trouble? It's like on kick returns—I don't believe I should ever get hit square on a kick return. It amazes me that guys will let themselves get racked up—here one minute and buried the next. With that much open field nobody should get more than a glancing blow on you."

*Running from scrimmage, though, people must hit you pretty hard.*

"You get hit. But I'll tell you something else I do. When I go out on the field I always look for the baddest dude on the other team and I get it in my mind that he's never going to hit me. Let Larry Csonka go looking for Dick Butkus to hit. When you challenge those guys, you win some and you lose some, and I don't like to lose."

*There again, a lot of people think that runners should establish themselves by going after the tacklers.*

"I know. A lot of guys have been brainwashed and they want to go after that big guy and feel good about taking him on head to head. But that's hard work, man, and I *play* football. I'm playing just like when I used to play on the sandlots back on Potrero Hill in San Francisco. I never lost a game back on Potrero Hill. If we were behind when it was getting dark, I'd just get moving and score a couple of times. That was fun and that's still how I play best, hanging loose and having a good time."

*What is your idea of running well? What do you think about when you're running?*

"Nothing. My definition of a good runner is that he's *insane*—he does wild things, stuff you never see, and he does it spontaneously. Even *he* doesn't know what he's going to do next. All I know is that when I'm running well, my mind just goes blank. I'm not thinking about anything at all. Thinking is what gets you caught from behind."

*You mean you are unconscious?*

"No, even though I'm not thinking, I'm aware of everything. I may run sixty yards

# "My definition of a good runner is that he's insane—he does wild stuff you never see."

without a thought, but when I get to the end zone I can tell you where everybody was, who blocked who. And I mean not just the guys near me, but all over the field."

*The Miami coach, Don Shula, has studied films of you for years and he says it looks like you can see out of the back of your head. You cut away from people coming up behind you.*

"Yeah, I've had people come up to me and say, 'Man, you must have ESP the way you run.' But that's not it either. Preparation is the key. Knowing what you're doing. A good analyst on Wall Street, he can predict the performance of certain stocks. Is that ESP? No. It's study and preparation, seeing the trends. You just have to do your homework."

*O. J. Simpson, the spontaneous genius-type, does it all with pre-game study?*

"I'll tell you what. At USC I used to carry the ball seventy times at every practice. Seventy times. Here in Buffalo, two-thirds of the time in every workout it's me carrying the ball. If you study the play design and then run the play enough in practice, you get to where you know where everybody is. Or at least you know where everybody *should* be. Bad teams can mess you up."

*What do you mean?*

"I think you'll see that I usually have my best games against the good teams. You watch the way we play Pittsburgh. And that's because Pittsburgh is good. They

have good players, players who know what their responsibilities are. They do the right thing. So I know where they are. It's the bad teams that drive you crazy. You never know *what* those guys are going to do. Against one of those teams once I broke off tackle and I had a touchdown. I *had* it. I cut outside just to get myself a little more breathing room, and I ran right into a guy. Crash. We looked at the films later and that guy was totally out of position. *Totally* out of position. The guy had gone for a fake so bad ten yards earlier that he was just stumbling around. He had no business being there. How can you bust one against people like that?"

*Assuming your opponents know what they are doing, are there any tips you have for breaking off the long run?*

"The key thing is to fake a guy tight."

*What do you mean by that?*

"Anybody can fake a guy if he uses the whole field. You just cut away and use the great circle route. But all you do then is run into more people. Or into the sideline. What you have to do is juke a guy without leaving him. Fake him but stay close to him. You just get him a little off balance and then blow right by him, where he can touch you but can't stop you. See, the whole idea is to get upfield right now. The goal line is upfield. You can't take long detours around everybody you see."

*O. J., most people think it takes more than preparation and athletic ability to make a great athlete.*

"Yes, it does. It takes character."

*That's what I was going to ask about. Do you think football builds character? What is character, anyway?*

"Well, now. That's a good question. I have a feel for it. I know it when I see it. But how do you define it? I think the best thing to say is that it's knowledge. Self-knowledge. When you see a man, and you see that he knows himself, he knows what's inside, that's where character starts."

*What do you mean exactly?*

"A man has to know his own abilities. He has to know what it takes to get the job done. He has to have been there and back, and know how he did it. That's when you can see the determination in a man, the force of will. Let's put it this way. A man of character knows what his limitations are—but he doesn't accept them."

*Can you put this in football terms?*

"Football is a stage. It's an arena where you will get an opportunity to express your character. There will come a time when you are tested, a point where you are so tired, so hurting, that you have to say, 'No, I can't. I can't go on.' Your body and your mind are both saying, 'I can't do no more.' "

*And what happens?*

"You *do* more. If you have character."

*Character is beyond the end?*

"If you get to your limit and you don't stop, you've got it. Or this is another way to put it: character is never saying 'No.' You dream the impossible dream, and you go after it."

*Where does character come from?*

"I don't know. Some guys have it. Look at Reggie McKenzie, my guard here in Buffalo. Talk about a guy with character. He doesn't know where 'No' is. We've had some tough times on this team. We've been beaten week after week. Still, every Sunday we go out there and Reggie says, 'We can *beat* these guys.' And he means it. And he gets other people to believe it."

# "Hey, my kid Jason is only nine years old, and he can make an excuse."

*And now you are winning.*

"It's no accident. You get people like that, you start winning."

*Do you think character is the winner's edge?*

"I've got an angle on that. I've had one basic philosophy all my life, even as a kid. What I believe is that the day you take complete responsibility for yourself, the day you stop making any excuses, that's the day you start to the top."

*Don't some people start at a disadvantage?*

"This is what I tell kids when I get a chance. Don't blame anybody else for what comes down on you. Whatever happens, you *let* it happen. You deserve it. So don't give me any excuses. Hey, my kid Jason is only nine years old, and he can make an excuse. Anybody can make an excuse. What you have to do is take responsibility for yourself. People try to say they don't have this advantage, they don't have that advantage. They say, I would have made it, but *he* did *this,* or *she* did *that,* or *whoever* did *whatever*. None of that means anything. If I didn't do it, I didn't do it. If I can't read, it's my fault. If I can't write, it's my fault. Don't talk about bad teachers or bad schools. It's me."

*Winners look to themselves?*

"That's what I'm saying. You never hear a real winner giving excuses in the locker room. 'I got beat.' It's simple. You show me a person like that, I'll show you somebody who, in the long run, is sure to be a winner. And I'll tell you something else, too. That's the kind of guy we've got playing in Buffalo now."

*The Bills have been losing for a long time.*

"Hey, that's over, man. Buffalo is a winning team starting now. We've got the coaches and we've got the players and we've got the attitude. When Saban first came here, he said something I thought was really important. He said, 'We don't make any excuses for ineptness. If a guy isn't playing well, you go up and tell him.' And on this club, that's what we do. We're always jiving each other about our play. 'Hey, I saw so-and-so really *tag* you,' somebody will say. 'Yeah, well, watch me put it on him this time,' the guy will answer. The thing is, we've got a young team and I think the guys take criticism from their peers really well. With the old kind of ballplayer, you told him he missed a block and you had a fight on your hands. But now we're always loose and ready. It's like the sandlots again, when Charley Norris would beat Don Crenshaw and we'd get on Donny's case good. 'Aw, sucker, you got beat. Can't you play?' And then Donny goes out and does it up the next play. It's a healthy attitude. It keeps people open and communicating and that's what we've got on the Bills now."

*Sounds like you are looking forward to the season.*

"I can't wait to get back to Buffalo."

# Joe Greene

**"Everybody is at the same intensity.
It's a super, super feeling."**

# Joe Greene

**"Boldness has genius, power, and magic in it."**

—*Goethe*

**T**here are few players so good an entire defense could be conceived and built around their talents. But there is Mean Joe Greene. This great Steeler defensive tackle comes out of his stance like a cross between a rabbit and Tyrannosaurus Rex. To make the most of this explosion, the Steelers have designed a defensive alignment that features Greene cocked inward at an angle, ready to go off in the earhole of the offensive center. As he batters into the heart of the offense, Greene pounds into two blockers, and often both of them together can't handle him. The whole offense is distorted and one or two other Steelers never get blocked at all. It's a wonderful defense, but you don't see other teams using it. Other teams don't have Mean Joe Greene.

If they did, however, they would find him to be more than a physical phenomenon. He is a deep and thoughtful man, a winner who leads by more than example. In this wide-ranging 1980 interview Greene reflects on his decade of pro football experience, a decade in which he has spearheaded four Super Bowl wins for the Steelers despite a severe and lingering nerve injury he first suffered in 1975. Greene discusses the challenge of having to remake his game after his injury. He also emphasizes the importance of the fans, analyzes the contribution of his coach, Chuck Noll, and goes into the topic of character even more thoroughly than O. J. Simpson. And for those interested in the Triangle of Success (see introduction), Greene is a lively source. Several of his key ideas might be placed under the categories of Strong Thought and Honest Assessment, for example. And as for Dynamic Action, a definition of all-out effort is the first thing Greene talks about when you ask him to identify the winner's edge. He starts off with a single word, one ringing word that sums his Texas background, the power he was born with, and the success he has known.

"In-TEN-sity."

*What do you mean by that?*

"There are many ways to view it. You are playing with every part of yourself. But it comes down to just this: the will to get the job done."

*How does it feel when you have it?*

"It's beautiful. It is beautiful. You are going all out. You are full of the desire to succeed. You are full of a feeling of power, of confidence, of *superior* confidence. You reach a peak in every part of your being. You reach an emotional high, a physical high, a mental high, all of them together. It's almost like being possessed."

*That sounds like action out of control. How can you keep command of yourself?*

# "Our intensity was so high it defies description. It beggars description."

"It's wild. It *is* a kind of frenzy, of wild action. But you are never out of control. You have great awareness of everything that is happening around you and of your part in the whole. You know that whatever is about to happen, it's going to turn out right. And it does."

*Can you think of any other experience in life that compares with it?*

"I really can't. It doesn't compare, particularly when the feeling is being transmitted, when it permeates the whole ball club. This is the ultimate. All eleven men on the defense are playing with peak intensity. You are surrounded with that frenzy. You know that you yourself are going to sell the farm on every play—you are going to give everything you have to give. And you know when you have *sold* the farm, when it's all gone and there's nothing more, somebody else is going to come in to finish up the job. Everybody is at the same intensity. It's a super, super feeling."

*How often is the whole defense playing at that level?*

"I think the Pittsburgh Steelers come closer to that level more often than any other team. On a scale of ten, maybe most teams are at a five or six in the big games. The Steelers are seven or eight. But there has only been one game where everybody was at a peak, where every man was at ten all at once. That one game is why I know what it feels like. It gives me a standard for comparison. It was the 1974 playoff game against Oakland."

*Why did that one game reach such a level?*

"This was for the AFC championship. And you have to understand that Oakland at that time was the dominant force in the AFC. They could destroy a team. They had just beaten Miami in a playoff game—a beautiful game—and one of their coaches said that it had been a showdown between the two best football teams in the league."

*Did you think so?*

"I wasn't sure. But during our week of preparation, our coach, Chuck Noll, let us know what he thought. 'We've got news for the Oakland Raiders,' he said. 'We are the best team in this league.'"

# "This is a particular moment in time, and you want to take advantage of it."

*That sounds like standard coach's talk, using a quote by the other team to psyche up his own players.*

"But you have to understand. Chuck Noll doesn't *talk* like that. We were just on our way up as a team, and the reason his statement had such magnitude is that he had never said anything like that before in his six years with the team. He's not boastful. He's not a braggart. He just said it as a matter of fact. 'We *are* the best team.' It took a lot of us by surprise to hear him talk like that, but it set our heads right. From that moment on, we *knew*. We had more intensity all week in practice than most teams have in a game. We just got into a state of mind as a team that it didn't matter what Oakland did, they were going down."

*And how did it feel during the game?*

"It was incredible. It defies description. It *beggars* description. The game was on Oakland's home field, in front of their fans, but our intensity was at such a high decibel level, it just didn't make any difference where we were. Oakland only got twenty-five yards running all day. They never had a chance. And Chuck Noll created that."

*You really feel your coach is that important?*

"It all comes back to Chuck. He isn't into hollering and screaming, but he's the man who creates the atmosphere. He's a master at getting things done without making a lot of noise. He doesn't run up to you and say, 'Joe, that was a tremendous play.'

But you will get a certain look, a little smile. He can communicate without uttering a word. He's the man who makes it happen. That intensity is there in all of us, but he has the ability to bring it out of you. No, better, he has the ability to make *you* bring it out."

*Is there anything else that accounts for Steeler intensity?*

"One thing is the talent on this ball club. There are some truly remarkable athletes here. It is a rare group. And you have the sense that it all can't last forever, that this is a particular moment in time, so you want to take advantage of every possible chance. You want to be a part of that group and stay a part of that group. You want to perform up to Lynn Swann's level, up to Jack Lambert's level, up to Mike Webster's level, up to Dave Stallworth's level. This is the standard that is being set."

*Is there anything else?*

"The fans. There is no doubt about it. The Steelers' history hasn't been all that beautiful, you know. The fans around here have known some moments of despair. But when they got the taste of a few victories, they just went wild. The way they pull for us is a determining factor in a lot of games."

*You think so? Pro football players are supposed to be immune to crowd reaction, positive or negative.*

"I used to think like that. I believed that pro ball was less emotional than col-

# "You run the gamut of life so fast. Your character is tested in the fire."

lege. I thought that, look, I'm a pro and it's my duty to go out there and play no matter how the fans are acting. But the fans here sure changed my head around. Football players are human, too, that's what I found out. We function on emotions, too. There might have been times in the past when the fans here were a little critical, and they had a right to be. But now, as soon as you step out on the field, the fans make you feel like you belong there. You walk out there and you just know it's going to be your day. It's like in golf, there are some days when you step up to the first tee and you can feel that you've got it, that you're going to play one fantastic round. That's how the fans make us feel every game in Pittsburgh. And any time things start to drag, they give us a shot in the arm. 'Dee-fense, Dee-fense,' they scream. And it does affect you. You can feel it jack you up. The fans can create their own intensity."

*When did you feel this Steeler team first came of age?*

"It's hard to pick out one point. That Oakland game sticks out. But you have to go awhile in this game to really mature. The first two or three years in the league, a player is really just a kid, regardless of talent. But for those who last, the growing up is quick. You run the gamut of life so fast in this game. There are so many highs and lows. Your character is tested in the fire."

*In what way?*

"You are continually confronted with new situations. The question is, how do

you deal with those situations? How do you deal with immediate failure? Say you get blocked out of a play. How do you handle that? How do you relate to success—a tackle, maybe, or a sack? How do you handle that? There are so many of these successes and failures in one ball game. Then there's the long haul—a season, a career. How do you deal with injuries? How do you handle yourself when someone is playing in front of you? You're a man, he's a man. How do you deal with that? And think now, all this testing doesn't go on behind closed doors. You're tested for the whole world to see."

*Let's take the example of failure. If a man has character, how should he handle that?*

"You take responsibility for it."

*That's the same point O. J. Simpson makes.*

"He's not a bad man to agree with."

*But what if a particular situation wasn't really your fault? Suppose on some play your foot just slipped or it was really the man next to you who broke down?*

"You can't look at things like that. Every play, you are the one that has to wear the hat. You have to make it happen. You have to take responsibility for yourself, and you have to take responsibility for your team."

*But why?*

"That's how you get better. You have to be critical of yourself. Not super critical, but you have to call the play as it is. Then

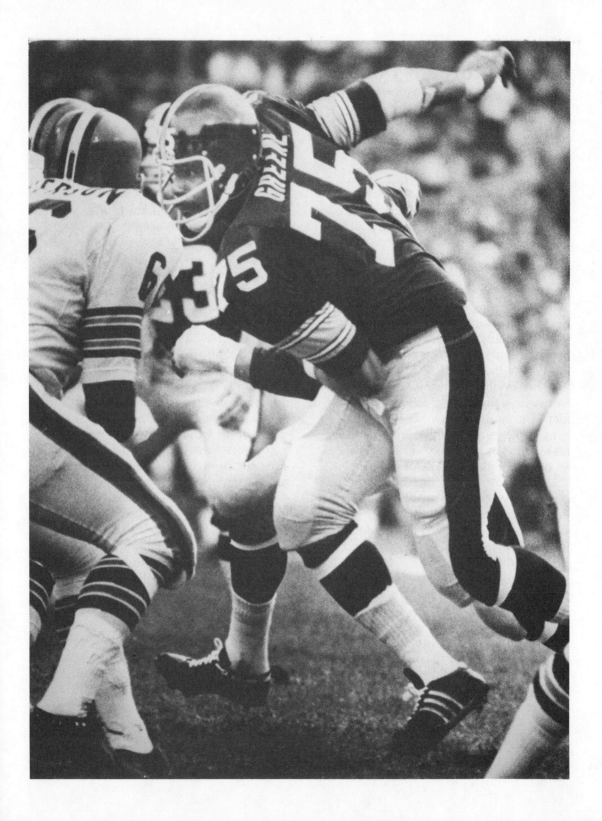

# "It's a game I'll never play. But it's a dream I enjoy chasing."

you can grow from there. If you make excuses for yourself, you're telling yourself that everything is really all right. You're going nowhere. You can't ever let yourself be satisfied. That's why, for the most part, the most useful competition is against your own self."

*How do you compete with yourself?*

"Personally, I imagine the ideal football player. Then I try for that."

*What's the ideal?*

"I'm a defensive tackle. The ideal would be a man who could do no wrong, a man who could beat two or three blockers consistently, a man who could make tackles sideline to sideline. An ideal tackle is an offensive player on defense."

*How close to the ideal have you come?*

"It's a game I'll never play. But it's a dream I enjoy chasing."

*We've talked about the attitude toward failure. Let's turn the question around. How should a man of character deal with success?"*

"It's simple, but it may not be easy. You need to hold clearly in mind that your success is not totally based on your own athletic prowess or your own intellectuality. It's based on your team's scheme of things. It's based on who you play with. And it's based on God."

*That seems . . .*

"Not necessarily in that order."

*That does seem a good thing to keep in mind. You yourself were obviously blessed with the physical and mental equipment of* a superb athlete. What has been the biggest challenge you have faced in your career?

"I'd have to say it was when my left side left me."

*When you had a problem with the nerve in your left shoulder and arm?*

"I still have some problem. I'm not all the way back physically, even though I was first hurt in 1975."

*And that was a major shock?*

"You have to realize my past. Until I was hurt, I always felt in control of the situation on a football field. I really hadn't been challenged many times. I felt I could do anything I wanted to out there. In fact, just before I got hurt, I thought I was about to break through onto a whole new plateau as far as my playing was concerned."

*Chuck Noll might have agreed. He called your three playoff games at the end of the 1974 season the best he had ever seen a defensive lineman have.*

"I appreciated that. But then it was just gone. My left side just disappeared. And that side is the lead side on every play. It makes the first contact. I thought I was about to set a new standard of play, and suddenly I could hardly hold my own. My coordination was bad. I was very weak. I lost control out on the field. It was a trying time."

*How did you respond?*

"The lowest point was 1975 and the training camp after that. I was playing before I was ready, and I couldn't get much done. But I was always confident. I knew I

# "You have to realize my past. I hadn't been challenged many times."

just had to take hold of that situation. The test was how well I would meet that particular challenge, and I wanted that test. As it turned out, what I had to do was change my whole style of play. I would have been foolhardy to try to mimic the way I moved before the injury. I had to learn new approaches, find pleasure in new things. And I was able to do that."

*What do you mean specifically?*

"I had to be content to be a back-up to other people on our defense. I couldn't always make the play myself, so I had to funnel the action toward my teammates. Fortunately, the other teams were still respecting me, still putting the blockers on me. So I figured as long as I could fool them and get the attention, I could help my team get the job done."

*Do you think that type of experience has made any change in your life?*

"Of course, there has definitely been a positive carry-over. In the first place, I had to learn the game of football much better. I had to get a thorough grasp of everything we were trying to do so I could fit myself into the pattern. The first year or two I was struggling. But by 1978 or so, I thought I was contributing more to Pittsburgh defense than I ever had. That's when I learned that the bottom line is *effectiveness*. It doesn't matter about flashy talent and all that. The question is, what do you get done? Not how do you do it, but what gets done? And in terms of effectiveness, I felt I was all the way back by '78. And I'm

# "I had to learn new approaches, find pleasure in new things."

getting closer physically, too. My left side is stronger every year. My goal is to get that back, too."

*Were there any other lessons?*

"The biggest one. I think that whole experience built a part of me. If a man has been accustomed to nothing but success, and then there is failure, it can be traumatic. But it brings out something good. You have to grow. You have to take hold of yourself. Before I was hurt, I never made any plans, for instance. I'd just get out on the field and play. I'd go with the occasion. But that's not the best way to grow. If you just haphazardly go through what you're doing, if you just let things happen, then a lot of things slide by that you don't recognize. But when I had to plan out what I was going to do, study up and find some way to help my team with only one side to work with, then I found a way to grow and progress. When you have plans, you can get into your history. You can chronicle your progress and reflect back on what's happened. Did I do what I planned? Why? Why not? You can check your progress. You have a measuring stick of how far you've come and how far there is to go. It keeps you growing. And that's a good thing. I can identify now with what Chuck says sometimes, 'You never arrive.' When you think you've arrived, you're going backward. The injury was a hard thing, but sometimes I can truthfully say I'm glad it happened."

*Football teams spend a lot of time watching game films. Do you think they really help you judge your play? Do they make you better?*

"They do the way they are used here in Pittsburgh. The films here are used in a positive way. Nobody is into tearing people down, taking liberties with their manhood. Criticism is always positive. It's about teaching. We review every game the following Tuesday, and that's how we check up on our effectiveness in sticking to our play. If there are mistakes, we find them. If we do it right, it feels very good to watch it."

*And you think that experience is important to winning football games?*

"We have to judge it as important. But one thing does definitely weigh more heavily in the balance."

*What's that?*

"In-TEN-sity."

# Dan Dierdorf

"Don't tell me what you did for me yesterday.
Tell me what you'll do for me tomorrow."

# Dan Dierdorf

**"Inspect the neighborhood of thy life,
every shelf, every nook of thy abode."**

*—John Paul Richter*

**O**n the third page of their press book
the St. Louis Cardinals let you know
what they think of Dan Dierdorf. On that
page is the first action photograph in the
book, one of only two they use, a big full-
page shot. And what it shows, front and
center with no one close to share the glory,
is Dan Dierdorf, offensive tackle.

Offensive linemen rarely get this kind
of billing, of course, but the offensive line
is rarely played the way Dan Dierdorf plays
it. He is a dominating force in the NFL. He
has been chosen All-Pro five times and,
even more impressively, he was chosen by
his fellow players as the outstanding offensive lineman in the National Football Conference for three consecutive years—until a
leg injury slowed him down in 1979.

At 6'3" and 288, Dierdorf is a giant
even in a world of big men. But when you
ask him about the winner's edge, it is not
size and strength he mentions. He talks at
length, instead, about mental strength,
about the scrimmage battles that take place
in consciousness, about the intense strug-
gles for psychological dominance. And
with even more emphasis, Dierdorf discusses his central point, the idea that championship athletes must keep constant tabs
on themselves. He is a strong advocate of
self-monitoring and self-analysis—what
Christopher Attwood calls Honest Assessment (see introduction).

"You have to take physical ability for
granted," says Dierdorf. "Everybody you
are talking to in this book has tremendous
physical talent. And everybody we play
against has great talent, too. So over and
above that what singles out the winners?
To me, it's pretty simple. If you want to
win and keep winning, it all comes down
to one thing. You have to pay strict attention—and I mean attention with a capital
'A'—to even the smallest details."

*What sort of details are you speaking
of?*

"Well, it's obvious there is nothing too
small to learn about your opponent. We
spend hours looking at films to find out
things about the people we are playing. But
in what I do, I think there is something
even more important."

*What's that?*

"Taking the time to study myself."

*How do you do that?*

"Here in St. Louis we take films of
every practice. On Tuesday they shoot us
practicing our pass blocking, let's say. On
Wednesday we come in and study those
pictures first thing in the morning. In fact,
we study films of ourselves every day of
the week."

*You have been playing pro football for
nine years now. You've been practicing the
pass block six months a year for all that
time. Don't you think you know how to do*

# "To win and keep winning, you have to pay attention to the smallest details."

*it by now? Why do you have to keep watching yourself over and over?*

"Let's just think about it for a minute. Setting up to pass block is a completely unnatural movement. It's unnatural to be moving backwards, with your legs bent just right, with your feet spread just far enough, with your weight neither too far back nor too far forward. It's unnatural, and every detail has to be just right. That defensive end is coming at you, and he's a big guy, a great athlete. He's just looking for you to make some mistake. If you get your feet too wide, he changes direction quickly and you can't recover. If you get your feet too close together, he bangs you on the shoulder and knocks you off balance. If your weight is too far forward, he pulls you and you tip over. If your weight is too far back, he comes right over the top of you. Pass blocking is like a precise dance step, and it has to be perfect time after time, game after game, when you are exhausted, when the ground is slop, whatever is happening. There's only one way I know to make sure that it is. You have to study yourself every day."

*Do all offensive linemen do this?*

"I don't think a lot of teams do this. In fact, I think some people think it's ridiculous. And I'll tell you the truth, it took me a long time to get comfortable with the idea myself. I was afraid I wasn't seeing enough film of my opponent. But Jim Hanifan kept with the idea. He was our offensive line coach then (he's the head coach now) and

he was firmly convinced that the first thing you should do is know yourself. And I'll tell you what. I'm a believer now. If I'm doing what I have to do, if I have the proper technique, if I don't make any mistakes, then I don't feel I can be beaten. I don't worry about the other guy. If my feet are right, if my balance is right, if my body line is right, there's nothing he can do. I can't be beaten."

*Still, it must be hard to keep working on the same details every day. You've made it to the top of your profession. Don't you find it hard to keep motivated?*

"No. No way. In fact, there's more motivation to maintain that status. Everybody is looking for you to lose a step. If everything isn't letter-perfect, they say you're slipping. There is no tendency to rest on your laurels. In pro football, there are no laurels. Don't tell me what you did for me yesterday. Tell me what you'll do for me tomorrow."

*Everybody you play must be gunning for you, too.*

"Yeah, when you get some reputation you're definitely the target of the people you play against. That's why I think the first couple of plays in every game are extra important."

*Why is that?*

"You have to realize that an offensive tackle is really playing a man-to-man game with only one guy, the defensive end. It may be the St. Louis Cardinals against the Los Angeles Rams, but for me its just Dan Dierdorf against Jack Youngblood. Even the guard next to me, working on the defensive tackle, it's not the same. If the guard's block starts to slip, he gets help from the center. But with me, I'm out there alone and there's a lot of room to work with. The defensive end may start two yards outside of me. He has a running start, and if I miss him, there's no help. It's straight to the quarterback. So when I take the field, it's strictly a one-on-one situation. And I think the most important thing one-on-one is to never let that man get started. Don't let him get any momentum, don't let him catch fire."

*How do you do that?*

"It starts physically, of course, but the key is the mind. If I can beat a guy in his mind, everything else falls into place. So the first thing, the first couple of plays, I'm super aggressive. I'm out of my stance and on the guy. I go out of my way to make him look bad, to notify him that if he's looking for a go-around, I'm ready. The thing is, unless I'm playing Youngblood or L. C. Greenwood, one of the great ones, then I'm definitely the favorite when the game starts. And in those first few plays I want to remove any hope from the guy's mind that maybe Dierdorf is going to have an off day, that he's not paying attention today. I want to establish that he's going to get manhandled. It's a question of establishing your territory. It's a basic human drive, even an animal drive. It gets across."

*And it's basically a question of strength, of aggressiveness?*

# "That's a crushing blow. His play may disintegrate for the whole day."

"Aggressiveness, yes, but it's all technique, too. All the energy in the world wouldn't be enough if the proper technique weren't there. You've got to study those films."

*But can you beat a guy down with technique? How can finesse dominate a man's mind?*

"Think about it this way. Here's a defensive end. He's heard about Dan Dierdorf. I like to think he's put in a long, hard week trying to learn how to beat me. Maybe he's been focusing on one particular move. His coaches have been trying to convince him, 'When you put this move on Dierdorf, you got him.' And he believes it, or he wants to believe it. It helps him put in the work in practice. Then comes the game, and he tries his big move, and you repel it easily. You've been spending the whole week working on yourself. You come in on Sunday and your techniques are razor sharp. And whatever he does you rebuff it easily, almost casually. Psychologically, that's a crushing blow. It's all over. His play may disintegrate for the rest of the day. And that's what I'm looking to do."

*These are professional football players. Can one play really take a man apart like that?*

"You wouldn't think so. It seems hard to imagine with players on a pro level. But some guys can be intimidated. And I don't mean intimidate like some of the cheap shot types, who take a thirty-yard running start at a receiver and cold-cock him. I'm not talking about mangling a guy physically. Line play isn't like that. But you can establish dominance, get on top physically, mentally, psychologically. And soon a lot of guys just stop hustling. They may go through the motions, make it look good. But you can't fool the guy you're playing against. You can see them with one eye on the clock, thinking, 'My God, I wish this game were over.' You've got his mind."

*What about the guys who won't quit?*

"The Youngbloods and Greenwoods. These are the football players. You can beat some guys to death play after play, but they never stop coming. You've got a four-quarter slugfest on your hands. That's when the game is really fun."

*You enjoy having to work so hard?*

"Don't get me wrong. I like to get a guy down early. But if you don't enjoy playing against the best, then you're one of the guys who get intimidated. Besides, playing against a guy you're supposed to beat, sometimes you can get too cautious. If I play against some rookie, I've got everything to lose. He's never supposed to beat me. If he gets by me for even one sack, I've had a terrible day. It's embarrassing. And worrying about that can make you so tentative, so cautious, that you're really playing just to keep from losing. It's not much fun. But if I'm up against a great one, then things are the way they ought to be. It's no embarrassment to get beat by a guy like that once in a while. So you go for it. All

# "There's an air of humility about players like that that I like."

the stops are out. Caution is to the wind, and you're battling with everything you have. That's the real fun of the game."

*Do you use emotion to psyche up for a man like that? Do you try to work up a hate for him?*

"You don't need that. I've got a great deal of respect and admiration for the great ones, the guys who never quit. I respect anybody who succeeds in this game because I know it's not easily done. And I especially appreciate the ones who do it with some style, some class."

*What do you mean by that?*

"You never hear Jack Youngblood run anybody down. He may get two or three sacks in one game, but all he talks about is the field was slippery or the other guy had an off day. He never calls anybody a dog. He never blows his own horn. There's an air of humility about players like that that I like. It's just a personal choice, but I admire it."

*Dan, you're only thirty-one, but you already have a thriving printing business in St. Louis to go with your All-Pro honors. Do you find that much of what you have learned in football makes a difference in the business world?*

"There's no doubt about it. There is a direct correlation between the two. In business, for instance, you have to take responsibility involving a lot of different people. You have to make deliveries for your customers on time. You have to take care of your employees. And if there is anything you learn playing football, it is that sense of responsibility to a variety of people—to your teammates, your coaches, even to the people in your community who make it all possible. So responsibility is one thing. Another thing is dedication and hard work. Printing, for instance, is a demanding business. You're on deadline all the time and you have to produce. I was in here until 11:15 last night. But I don't mind. I like hard work. Football helped with that. But to me the main lesson is the one we started out talking about."

*Focusing on yourself and what you are trying to do?*

"Exactly. I take the same approach in business that I do in football. I think a lot of people get too concerned with their competition. They fall into the habit of worrying about everyone else. But I just don't pay attention to what others are doing. I feel strongly that if I've got correct goals, and if I keep pursuing them the best way I know how, everything else falls into line. If I'm doing the right thing right, I'm going to succeed."

*Regardless of anyone else?*

"Regardless. I can't be beaten."

# Roger Staubach

**"Confidence comes from hours and days and weeks and years of constant work and dedication."**

# Roger Staubach

**"Nature suffers nothing to remain in her kingdom which cannot help itself."**

—*Emerson*

**V**ery few athletes come out of the service academies and go on to star in pro football. After graduating from Annapolis or West Point, a player must put in four long years of military service before pro ball becomes possible. Only one man has done it in recent times. But he is no ordinary athlete. He is Roger Staubach, the Dallas Cowboy quarterback of the 1970s.

Not only did Staubach make the transition from Navy life to the NFL. He also went from the most famous wild-hair scrambler in football history—Roger the Dodger of circuitous fame—to a stolid, strong-armed, pocket-loving passer. By the time of his retirement he was the NFL's top-ranked passer of all time, and he led his team from a desert of big game losses to the promised land of two Super Bowl wins.

But the definitive fact about Roger Staubach is that he loved to play in the clutch. In those last few seconds he carried the load as well as anyone who ever played, and his Cowboy career was punctuated by many gallant, last-gasp rallies. In his decade-plus of play he generated twenty-three come-from-behind victories in the fourth quarter, fourteen of them in the last two minutes or in overtime.

When you ask him for the most valuable asset of a come-back quarterback, Staubach discusses a characteristic twist. It seems obvious that powerful and positive thinking can lead to effective action, but Staubach makes the point that the right kind of action, and enough of it, can also lead back toward solid, unshakeable thought. In an interview that dates from his final season, 1979, he starts this point by naming the most important requisite for clutch heroics.

"Confidence," he says.

*That's all?*

"It's the start. You can't do anything without it."

*But how do you get confidence?*

"This is the question. You can't become confident just by talking about it. You can't say, 'Now I'm going to be confident,' and have any hope for success. Confidence doesn't come out of nowhere. It's the result of something."

*What's that?*

"Hours and days and weeks and years of constant work and dedication. When I'm in the last two minutes of a December playoff game, I'm drawing confidence from wind sprints I did last March."

*Exercise that you did in the spring? How can that help you in December?*

"Exercise is good for you any time, of course. You always get some value from loosening up and doing some running. And if an athlete keeps himself in shape all year round, then everything goes easier for him.

# "I'm ready. I'm completely ready. And I know I'm ready. That's confidence."

But the most important part isn't physical, it's mental."

*How can exercise help your mental attitude?*

"The point is this: if I've spent all year—and many years—getting myself ready, if I've kept my body in shape, and worked on all the passes, and studied up' on all the defenses we see, then I'm ready. I'm completely ready. And I know I'm ready. That's confidence."

*So the basis of confidence is . . .*

"Hard work. There isn't any substitute. Some guys may get by for a little while on sheer ability, but if you want to stay on top, you have to like the work."

*What if you don't?*

"I found out what happens from no work in 1974. That whole spring I couldn't run at all because I had a bad ankle. Finally, they operated June 1, and it was two more months before I could really maneuver. Then the first thing that happened in the pre-season was I broke my ribs. By the opening game of the year I was in there, but I hadn't done much for nine months. And I had my worst slump ever, ten interceptions in four games, something like that."

*You had excuses, of course.*

"It did take me half that season just to get in shape, but what I'm saying is that in that situation, I had nothing to base confidence on. If I threw an interception, I was stuck. I couldn't look back to last week's practice where I threw many good passes because I hadn't yet. I couldn't look back to last summer where I had worked hard on the fundamentals because I'd missed nearly everything. I hadn't even run a step in the spring. I hadn't done anything, so I had no results."

*Which means?*

"No confidence."

*So all anybody needs to do is work hard?*

"Well, there is the matter of talent, of course. Some guys could put in a billion hours and never complete a sideline pass. We each have our own skills. But from there on, it's that self-discipline."

*Do you feel that your experience with the Navy helped you in this regard?*

"Yes, I do. My years at the Academy taught me the self-discipline, for sure. And then, in my four years of service, I had some jobs with responsibility, jobs with 100 people working for me. I didn't come into the responsibility of pro quarterback with no preparation."

*Were those the main values of your Navy years?*

"Those, and the working out I did. I had it in mind to play pro ball. I worked out for four years."

*Most service academy athletes lose their edge before they get their crack at the pros. Four years is a long time. When they finally get out, they are twenty-six or twenty-seven and rusty.*

"It's true. It could slip away. But I wasn't going to let it. I had a regular exer-

## "It's a circle. Work and confidence, and more work and more confidence."

52

cise schedule—running, lifting weights, and so on. And sometimes I'd just be sitting around the house with my wife, maybe ten at night, and suddenly the thought would hit me, 'I want to play pro ball.' And I'd just have to say something to Marianne, and go out running."

*That's a great picture: the future All-Pro, waiting four years, running through the night to keep himself ready.*

"It just felt so good. You get out there and run, and break a sweat, and the confidence comes right up. You can do it, and you can feel it, and the work is making it possible. It's just a circle: work and confidence and more work and more confidence."

*That backlog of readiness must make it much easier now.*

"It does in one sense. But you have to keep it up. You have to keep going. Football is amazing. You don't even have much time to enjoy the wins."

*You don't have any fun?*

"That's not what I mean. I like the work. And the night of a game, we usually have some friends over and enjoy our victory, if we had one—and fortunately, in Dallas, we usually do. Monday, too, you can still enjoy Sunday. But by Tuesday, it's gone. I just shove it out of my mind. There's meetings, and a new game plan to master. I have to give myself over to the new game completely. Otherwise where will I get my confidence next Sunday?"

*It's the same if you lose?*

"The same thing. The first day-and-a-half are the worst. But then you get that new chance. I just use the routine of the week to pull myself into the right attitude. In fact, by mid-week, a loss last Sunday can add to the enjoyment. You work extra hard, get into it more, because you can't wait to get out there and wipe out that memory, get even, start winning again."

*Football coaches used to say that football builds character. That's a passé attitude in some circles now. Do you believe it?*

"I don't think there's any doubt about it. In the first place, football teaches the team concept—working together, helping each other. And then you have to learn the self-discipline, the sacrifice, and just the plain perseverance. Nothing is automatic in football. There are ups and downs. But you learn to keep going, not to get thrown off by temporary changes. Look at a guy like Drew Pearson. He was a free agent. He had to do it on his own. Without perseverance, he wouldn't even be here."

*And you think this character building helps you in other parts of life?*

"I don't see how it couldn't. There are some guys, I know, who learn the lessons of football but they don't apply them elsewhere. They do it, but I don't see how. I think that growing up with sports has to help anybody."

# Jack Youngblood

### "You have to decide if the experience you will have is worth the pain you will feel."

# Jack Youngblood

"And have you not received faculties which will enable you to bear all that happens to you? Have you not received greatness of spirit? Have you not received courage? Have you not received endurance?"

—*Epictetus*

**J**ack Youngblood plays defensive end like one of those rooms in an Edgar Allen Poe story—the type with a floor that slowly squeezes up toward the ceiling. Play after play Youngblood just keeps turning the pressure higher. The Los Angeles Ram captain has been an All-Pro every year since the middle 1970s, but it wasn't until last December, in the first playoff game of 1979, that the general populace found out what his fellows have long known. You can't get Jack Youngblood to quit.

Playing in that game against Dallas, Youngblood got scissored, high-low, by two blockers. Something had to give. It was the fibula in his left leg, the smaller of two bones extending from knee to ankle. A broken bone would give most people pause, and it did Youngblood, too. He paused five plays, to be precise, while the flying hands of Los Angeles trainers swathed his left ankle in three pounds of adhesive tape. Then he was back on the field. Fitted with a plastic brace around his ankle, and taking nothing stronger than aspirin, Youngblood played on through the

NFC championship game against Tampa Bay and the Super Bowl against Pittsburgh. The Rams surprised the world with their Super Bowl show, and a large part of the reason was the inspiration they drew from their gutty leader.

Youngblood's heroics also summed up one truth of his sport. For professional football players the challenge to human achievement is often condensed into the obvious reality of physical pain. Major decisions are telescoped into one moment of truth: Can I play?

This insistent, immediate reality of pro football life can cause outsiders confusion. Some people tend to idolize athletes who play in pain, as though physical courage were more important than, say, being a good father or writing excellent poetry. On the other hand, some people think any athlete who plays hurt is a mindless brute sacrificing his body to a macho ideal. The truth, of course, is somewhere between. Pro football players are huge people with powerful, fully-formed bodies. Unlike a young athlete, who needs to protect a growing body, or the man in the street, who may not be equipped to handle a hangnail, the mature pro is a magnificent physical specimen for whom it is sometimes simply true that pain is a question of character and courage rather than bodily incapacity. For this select group of people, playing hurt can be a legitimate test.

Most of the rest of us may lack the physical equipment to play football with a

# "They wanted to look at it, but I told them, 'No, just tape it up.' "

broken bone, but that's not the important point in any event. The key is not *what* these men do, but *how*. Their specific feats may not translate to a less warrior-like life, but their underlying mechanics may have meaning for anyone. This at least seems the case with Jack Youngblood. When you ask him how he rose to his challenge, his answer has a broad application.

"It's all up to the mind," he says. "It's a question of whether you can control your intelligence."

*What can the mind do when a bone is snapped in half?*

"Well, first let's be clear that I didn't do anything idiotic when I played on that leg. The large bone, the tibia, is the one that carries all the weight for the leg, and I didn't hurt that. You break the tibia, you're in the hospital. But the fibula, the small bone, is just kind of hanging on the outside of the shin. If you break that you can do something about it."

*When did you know the bone was broken?*

"Right at the time. I heard it go. It snapped like a pencil. For a minute I was rolling around out there, moaning and groaning like a fish out of water. But as soon as I stood up and saw that my leg could support me, I knew what the situation was. When I went to the sideline they wanted to look at it, but I just told them, 'No, just tape it up.' I knew right then what the doctors told me after they X-rayed it at half time. If we supported it so it wouldn't

move, I wasn't going to make the original injury any worse. So then it was pretty simple. It was just a question of pain."

*And the mind can make pain go away?*

"Maybe, but mine didn't. That was some serious pain. I could run straight ahead all right, but when I tried to push off the left leg and drive inside, I could really feel it. And that's my best move. That's how I play. It was ironic when we finally reached the Super Bowl, to have reached the epitome of what I'm supposed to be doing as a football player, and here I had to play with a broken leg."

*But you said it was all up to the mind.*

"Your leg is still broken, you still can feel the pain. What I mean is that if you can control your intelligence, you can focus your attention where you want it. You can pay attention to the playing instead of the hurting. You get out there and start to play and you get so entranced by your job, by what you're supposed to be doing, that you forget about the pain. The conscious flow is all wrapped up in your activity. There's nothing left over for pain. Then only one thing can stop you."

*What's that?*

"Sometimes your body will just quit on you. You're rushing the passer, the guy's right there, you plant that left leg, and it just goes dead on you. Nothing happens. You may not be paying attention to the pain, but the body is only going so far."

*Now the question many people have is this: why put yourself through all that?*

# "You get so entranced by your job that you forget all about the pain."

"Here's how I see it. You are living a certain part of life, and you have a choice. You are hurt and a championship game is coming up. And you have to ask yourself, what is a game like that worth? You have to decide if the experience you will have is worth the pain you will feel."

*And you decided in favor of the experience.*

"We were going to the Super Bowl. How many football players ever get there? That wasn't any time to sit down—if there was any way I could play."

*As it turned out, did you think the experience was worth it?*

"I'll tell you it was. Even just coming out on the field was one of the most amazing experiences I ever had in my life. The championship of the world. Your whole career has come up to this day. It was almost spooky, the level of emotion was so high. It was almost crazy. I don't think I ran out there. I think I floated."

*And you had to feel good afterward, as well as the Rams played.*

"You kidding? We were totally ticked off. *Totally* ticked off. We knew we could beat the Steelers. We had 'em. Then two plays and they got away. But I wouldn't trade the experience I had that day for anything."

*Several times you have used the phrase "control of the intelligence." Can you explain that in more detail?*

"When you talk about a man's mind, I think there are two factors involved. One is the type of intelligence a man has. Does he have understanding? Can he comprehend the whole situation he's faced with? And does he have common sense, street sense? Then there is the more important question. Can he control the intelligence he has? Can he get the most out of his mental abilities? You can have all the intelligence in the world, be Phi Beta Kappa, collect college degrees, and it means nothing if you can't control it."

*What do you mean by control?*

"One thing is the ability to concentrate.

# "All the intelligence in the world means nothing if you can't control it."

Not everybody has learned how to concentrate. And a lot of people don't even known they *can't* concentrate. They go to a meeting, for instance, and they sit there. They come out thinking they know what went on just because they were in the same room with it. But that's no good. You have to know how to take information in, how to handle it and make it function. It's a skill you learn."

*You think concentration can be learned?*

"I know it can. I've learned a lot about it just since I came to the Rams, especially how to concentrate on the field, how to forget the past and ignore the future and just deal with what's happening right now. Merlin Olsen was still playing defensive tackle with the Rams my first few years, and he taught me a lot of things. You ought to ask him about it."

*Are there any other ways to learn "control of the intelligence"?*

"I'll tell you one thing I do. I visualize things in my mind before I have to do them. It's almost like I'm dreaming."

*Can you explain that?*

"Let's say I'm out driving. You spend a lot of time on the freeways in southern California, and it gives you time to think. I'll be sitting there in traffic and I'll imagine the game coming up. I'll visualize what the offense is throwing at me. I'll pick out specific instances, like the way the tackle in front of me sets up to pass block. Then I'll picture myself rushing in, making

a certain move on that tackle, getting around him. I'll play the whole game that way, in my mind. That's why I say it's like dreaming."

*How does that help you?*

"It's like having a mental workshop. You can practice what you want to do even when you can't go through it physically. You get comfortable with what you are doing in advance. By the time you are out there on Sunday, it's almost like *déjà vu*. You've been there before. You know what you want to do. So you just get after it. It's like you program your mind for success."

*Do you think that a "mental workshop" can help someone even outside of football?*

"Yes, I think there is a lot to be said for it. I know it does a lot for me. Just recently I had a meeting with mortgage brokers down in Florida. We want to build a couple of racquet ball clubs down there like the one we have here in California. Riding down on the airplane, I tried to visualize how that meeting would go. I didn't know what the men looked like, but I had talked to them on the telephone, and I knew what the considerations were. So I just went through everything I wanted to say, then I tried to imagine all the questions they might bring up, all the different possibilities there were for that deal. And I think that helps a lot. When a question comes up in the meeting, you just say, 'Yeah, right,' to yourself because you're on top of it. You know what to say. Since the other side may not have gone through that kind of prepara-

# "By the time you are out there on Sunday, it's almost like deja vu."

60

tion, it has to lend you more credibility. It keeps you a step ahead."

*So control of the intelligence doesn't come accidentally.*

"No way. It's something to work on just like you work on getting your body in shape. There are a lot of different things you can do. There are certain things you read about or hear about—techniques you might try. And I think if you take some of these to heart, you can find some things that will lend you a hand."

*And how does this all relate to the specific situation of your broken leg?*

"If you have practiced at controlling your intelligence, then you can adjust to changes. You know the type of thing you have to do. With a broken bone in your leg, there are some things you just can't do physically. You have to find those limitations, and then narrow your focus down and play a more controlled game within those limitations."

*How broad is your focus usually?*

"Usually when I'm down in my stance, I'm keeping track of a lot of things at once. I know where the ball is, so I can start when it moves. I keep track of the tackle in front of me, the tight end outside me, the offensive back on my side. You have a broad focus that takes in the whole operation in front of you, and you are keyed to react to the whole pattern. You want to give them problems wherever they attack. But when I got hurt, I had to focus down on just a few specifics. I wasn't fast enough

to react to the whole pattern, so I narrowed down to just the tackle in front of me, and maybe the tight end. I had to control my game within those boundaries and play a lot smarter. Maybe I couldn't make all the plays I usually do, but by controlling my play within my limitations, I could hold up my end. I could channel my game and do well in that one area. I could play an intelligent game and help the defense."

*It sounds like quite a challenge*

"It is. But this whole game is a challenge. It's so demanding, physically, emotionally, mentally. And pro ball gets better every year. To even survive in this league, you have to keep going, keep improving. It takes physical preparation, mental preparation, physical toughness, mental toughness. It takes your body, your mind, your character. You have to learn how to control all facets of your game. If you don't—if you get lost in the spin—eventually you just get cast aside like chaff."

*That seems bleak.*

"But it teaches you a useful lesson. You learn to measure up. You learn that, whatever you are doing in life, obstacles don't matter very much. Pain or other circumstances can be there, but if you want to do a job bad enough, you'll find a way to get it done. I honestly believe that if a man has talent, and he learns how to control his intelligence and direct that talent, the sky is the limit."

# Merlin Olsen

**"This doesn't mean I play perfect football every play. But I try."**

# Merlin Olsen

**"The virtue of a man ought to be measured not by his extraordinary exertions but by his everyday conduct."**

—*Pascal*

It's no surprise to those who have known him that Merlin Olsen has become one of the most respected television commentators in sports. He has always been one of the most articulate men in football. This doesn't fit the stereotype for defensive tackles. But then, at 6'5", 270, Olsen doesn't fit any restrictions too well.

For a decade and a half, Merlin was the solid center for a succession of top-flight defensive lines on the Los Angeles Rams. He was too strong to attack directly and too smart to trick. Moreover, there were those who watched him through his whole career without ever seeing him take a cheap shot.

His on-field success was due, in part, to his sheer physical equipment, but as this mid-70s interview shows, it was his mental discipline that kept him on top. Roger Staubach and Jack Youngblood have already indicated that strong thought is no accident, and here Olsen gives the recipe for concentration that he taught to Youngblood, a recipe that made him a model of day-after-day and play-after-play excellence in action. (Note: This interview appears by courtesy of the family's best writer, my father, Bob Oates, Sr., and is from his forthcoming book, *Forty Years of Winners*.)

Merlin Olsen, 32, is known to his peers as the most strikingly consistent football player in the game's history. In eleven years as a defensive tackle for the Los Angeles Rams, Olsen has been voted into eleven Pro Bowls. No one else has been good enough and durable enough to make the all-star game more than nine times.

The extraordinary thing about Olsen, as certified by those he plays for and against, is that under five Ram coaches—a new one about every two years—he has never had a bad season or even a bad game or hardly a bad play. When asked to discuss this perpetual excellence, he begins by listing four qualities.

"I'd say luck, determination, concentration and skill."

*In terms of the Pro Bowl every year, which is most important?*

"First, you can't be hurt. You more or less have to play every game all season, which takes a little luck. But the key to this thing—the key to consistency of performance—is concentration. I've probably held my ability to concentrate over a longer period of time than some athletes."

*What do you mean by concentration? What have you concentrated on these last eleven years?*

"Each game, at the beginning of each new play, I think of it as the most important play of the year. I go into it as if the game depends on it."

*Regardless of whether the Rams are far ahead or far behind?*

# "At the beginning of each play, I think of it as the most important of the year."

"Yes. If you have any lapses you start to slide immediately, and you may not even be ready next week."

*In a lopsided game, how do you convince yourself that a fourth quarter play is important?*

"I don't think about the preceding play, or the following play, or anything else. I approach every play as if it's an individual, distinct incident—a complete little game of its own. I consider a new play to be not only a separate situation but a new challenge. This doesn't mean I play perfect football on every play. But I try."

*Have you always known this instinctively or did you learn it?*

"I had to learn it. In fact, one of the first things I learned is that if you don't completely involve yourself in every play, you suddenly find you've lost it. If you take it easy for ten minutes, it takes a long time to get it back, sometimes a week or two. Like everything else, concentrating is a habit."

*If concentrating on every play explains your consistency, and if concentrating is a matter of habit, I assume you've worked out a routine you go through. Do you have a set of habits—a process?*

"I certainly do. After each play I think about the next one using a simple little system. First I tell myself the down and distance, then our position on the field, then I mentally review the tempo of the game. After those three things, I recall what I know—or what I've learned during the week—about what the other team likes to do in this particular situation."

*What do you do at that point?*

"I clear all those things out of my mind and prepare myself for the play."

*You habitually tell yourself the down and distance and then forget it?*

"Yes, I shove it completely out of my mind. It's like putting material into a computer. You don't have to keep reminding a computer what it knows. The difference between the human mind and a computer is just that the computer can't be distracted,

# "If you take it easy for ten minutes, it can take two weeks to get it back."

and that's what I'm trying to achieve. No distraction. I've reviewed the most probable two or three things the other team will do in every situation, but I don't try to out-think the other team. Computers don't guess and I don't want to guess either. I program the computer and then I just react. As the other team's play develops I'm *cued* by what they do to *react* to what they do."

*How do you stop the thinking process you were going through between plays?*

"I talk to myself."

*About what?*

"At the start of a play I say just the most obvious things. If it's third and twelve, I'm thinking: 'Off with the ball, get to the quarterback.' If it's fourth and one on our five-yard line, I think: 'Off with the ball, hold them.' "

*Do you always begin by reminding yourself to go with the snap of the ball?*

"Right. The only thing that comes ahead of that is a correct stance. Well begun is half done."

*You've been in the game a long time. Don't you find it difficult to focus on each play as if it's the most important of the year?*

"It's not terribly hard. Athletes differ, of course, and those who can sustain their concentration last longer than others. It starts with love of the game."

*Who would you single out as an exemplar of concentration?*

"Maybe the best was John Unitas. You couldn't shake him."

# "The thing that drives a real pro is simply inner satisfaction. That's all."

66

*How could you tell?*

"Once in a while the defense would get there, knock him down, stomp him, hurt him. The test of a quarterback is what he does next. Unitas got up, called another pass, and dropped back into the pocket. Out of the corner of his eye he might have seen you coming sometimes. And I swear that when he did, he held the ball a split second longer than he really needed—just to let you know he wasn't afraid of any man. Then he threw it on the button."

*Merlin, you were a member of one of the great defensive lines in recent history, the Fearsome Foursome. What did you think of that unit?*

"It was a pleasure to be associated with such a fine group of gentlemen."

*Could you describe each of them, in terms of their football abilities?*

"Next to me, at tackle, was Rosy Grier at first, and then Roger Brown. They were outstanding men to have in the middle, huge people who could move well. Then at right end was Lamar Lundy. Lamar was one of the most intelligent men in the game. And Lamar was consistent. He was there, play after play. And then, of course, there was the Deacon."

*In Los Angeles they used to call Deacon Jones the Secretary of Defense.*

"With reason. He was the best defensive end I've ever seen. Gino Marchetti had that tremendous effort on every play, but the Deacon was everything you could want in a defensive end, and then so fast on top of it. He would catch sweeps going the other way just as routine. In a way it was frustrating to play next to him."

*Why was that?*

"He was so fast he'd take most of the hits. I'd just be lining someone up when all of a sudden the guy would be down with Deacon on top of him. Sometimes I felt like asking him to leave some for other people."

*Jones was earning good money, of course. Do you think that had much to do with his zeal?*

"It's hard for people to understand that dollars don't have much to do with the way a pro plays. I have never met a real pro who felt that money could make up for the price he pays in effort, concentration, and total dedication. If you had offered Joe Greene $5000 for every tackle he made in the fourth quarter last Sunday, he would have made the same tackles you saw and no more."

*The ability for all-out concentration can't be bought?*

"What I'm saying is this: The thing that drives a real pro is simply inner satisfaction. That's all. And any real artist will know what I mean."

# Joe Namath

"I prepare myself until I know I can do what I have to. Then I have faith."

**"Success is the child of audacity."**

*—Disraeli*

H e was the $400,000 quarterback, Joe Willie Whiteshoes, doing what he wanted and making it stick by doing it well. No single athlete has ever had such a profound impact on his sport, though others have arguably played it as well. Joe Namath was not just a quarterback; he was a living revolution in the way to be an athlete. He stayed up late when he wanted to and told the truth when you asked him. He wasn't always loved, but he always got attention, and in the biggest game of his life he delivered masterfully—Super Bowl III in Miami.

His was a trying career in many ways: bitter controversies when he was on top, then a succession of injuries that dragged him down to anti-climactic second-string status in his last season with the Los Angeles Rams. But when he was asked in that last year if it was the worst experience of his life, he summed up his attitude when he said, "It could be, but I'm not going to let it be. I'm just going to accept it as a great experience. I went through things emotionally I never went through before. I'm a wiser man."

At the peak of Joe's career I had the privilege of doing a book with him on the topic of quarterbacking. The title was *A Matter of Style.* The following conversation

is drawn from that book (with the kind permission of Little, Brown, and Company), and it covers a broad range of topics—from the benefits of football on the personality to the complex and sometimes perplexing joys of teamwork. As a quarterback, however, Joe naturally puts much of his attention on the topic of athletic psychology. He agrees with, and elaborates on, Roger Staubach's point that preparation builds confidence, for instance. He also makes an intriguing observation: in some cases mental weakness and inertia can be overridden by speeding up the pace of thought. Like many machines, apparently, the mind can put out more power at higher RPMs. In addition, Namath defends the training concept he made famous. Relaxing is as important as working, he says. Easing up is as important as bearing down.

At the start of the interview, moreover, he honestly expresses one basis of the winner's psychology: the need for self-respect, for acceptance and approval by oneself and by others. If you ask him why he tried for the tackle that resulted in his last knee operation for instance—a tackle on an interception in a meaningless pre-season game—he even has a little trouble controlling his temper.

"Now I don't want to seem like I'm being wise or anything," he says, "but that's a dumb question. A lot of people have asked it, but it's still a dumb question. Did you ever play any football?"

*Not that people noticed.*

# "The adrenalin starts pumping. It's a whole other world on the football field."

"When you're out there on the field, there's a game going on. If some guy is trying to run past you and score a touchdown, you tackle him, that's all. How would you feel if one of your teammates stood there and watched some guy go by with the ball? I know how I'd feel. I'd tell the dumb sucker to get the hell off the field if he didn't want to play. And it's not only the guys on your team you're thinking about but also your family and the people you know. A player has to have self-respect."

*It makes a difference what other people think?*

"There's a story our coach, Paul Bryant, used to tell us at Alabama. One time he was talking to one of his teams in the locker room before a game. 'Now, damn,' he says.'Y'all going to run all over this team here. This team can't beat you. They're not *supposed* to beat you. They ain't got families near as good as your families. Their mommas and daddies ain't near as good as your mommas and daddies. Y'all just a better class of folks than they are. Now y'all ain't going to go out there and let your folks down, are you?'

"When Coach Bryant got through with his speech, the Aggies ran out and beat that team something awful. It was really bad. After the game the TV guys came in and they got a couple of the heroes for that day and put them up on the stand and the announcer asked one of the guys, 'Why did you do so well out there today?' He stuck the microphone in the player's face and the guy said, 'Because we got better mommas and daddies than they do.'"

*Still, you've been unlucky. I'm sure it would be more fun if you had two good knees. Do they bother you much off the field?*

"I don't move around too quickly most of the time. Sometimes I can't even get up

# "You do your best on the job, then you don't have to worry about it."

out of the chair. My leg will get stiff and I'll have to ease it around and bend it slowly."

*Yet out on the field you seem to move quite quickly.*

"That's different. When I'm throwing a football everything is all out, full speed. The adrenalin starts pumping and everything just feels quick and sharp, everything happens immediately, right now. You go back, look and Boom! The ball's gone. It's a whole other world on the football field."

*It sounds as if you enjoy playing the game.*

"Talking about playing quarterback, boy, quarterback is a gas. It's a hell of a position to play. It's a big responsibility, a challenge, and I like that. I get a lot of self-satisfaction out of it. First off, you have to be a pretty damn good athlete to be quick enough, have the right footwork and a good arm, have good enough reactions. And then you have to be able to handle the tactics, call the right plays in the right situations, keep calm under pressure and keep your team together and working. It's fun moving down the field and getting points on the board. I get a charge out of it."

*Quarterback is a big responsibility, however. Doesn't it worry you at all?*

"Not much. I hardly ever worry. I don't like it. I don't like the feeling of worrying, where your stomach is hurting and your mouth feels strange and your head's in a bad place. That's a bad feeling and I try to avoid it now. In the past, I did worry

# "I have to gear my mind up in stages, the same way I do my body."

73

sometimes. I can remember times when it was really rough. Did you ever lose money that you couldn't afford to lose? I did that a couple of times when I was in school and, buddy, that's a bad feeling. It was just twenty or thirty cents, but it was money I was supposed to bring home.

"My mother sent me out to the store and it was change, and on the way home I'd go into the pool hall and a couple of times I lost it. I'd be walking home and my stomach would really be doing it to me, and all I could hope was that they'd forget about the change. But I knew they wouldn't. That was a bad way to feel, worrying like that."

*Nobody likes to worry but a lot of times it's hard not to.*

"If you don't like it, why do it? It doesn't help you perform. In fact, it gets in your way. I think that at some point in your life you realize you don't have to worry if you do everything you're supposed to do right. Or if not right, if you do it the best you can. You have a job and you do your best on the job, then you don't have to worry about it. What can worry do for you? You are already doing the best you can.

"Sometimes I'll be at a party and I'll be sitting there, and I'll catch myself thinking about the game coming up or some business conference I've got. But as soon as I catch myself, I just put it away. Why do I want to be worrying when I'm at a party? If I've already got my game plan down or my business options clear, why think about the situation until I'm confronted with it?"

*Some people think that to succeed you need to keep your mind on the job all the time.*

"I know there are people who work like that. But it doesn't make sense to me. Once I know what I'm going to do I don't see any reason to eat, sleep and drink it. You just get yourself in knots, do it to your stomach. What I do is prepare myself until I know I can do what I have to do. Then I have faith."

*Some people might think you don't like hard work.*

"Well, there's something to that. Usually I don't do anything hard. A hard job for me is a job I don't like doing, and I try to keep that kind from coming up. But I don't mind working if I like what I'm doing—and I happen to like the game of football."

*What about during a game? Do you try to keep from fretting when the other team has the ball?*

"Yes, it's the same. If I'm prepared, I don't think about what I'm going to do until I have to do it. Sometimes I'll be on the sideline and the other team will be lining up to punt and a coach will come over and ask me what play I'm going to run on first down. Heck, I'm not even thinking about it yet. I don't know where the ball will come down, which hashmark it will be on, whether my guy might run it back thirty yards. Maybe one of their defensive backs

# "I usually need four games before
I've got my mind going at the speed I want."

74

will get hurt covering the kick. I don't
know the situation yet so I'm just waiting."

*And not worrying.*

"I don't call plays I have to worry
about."

*Still, quarterback is a demanding job.
Is there anything to do that lightens the
load of responsibility?*

"The best thing I know is just to know
your job and get control of it. Have complete confidence in what you're doing."

*How do you know if you have com-
plete confidence?*

"If you're not afraid to gamble in any
situation. If you can go ahead and throw
for six points any time you see an
opening."

*That must come easily now that you've
spent so many years in the pros.*

"The fact is, I have to start over every
year. Talking physically, every year I go
back to the basics about throwing the ball
and work the whole throwing motion up
from the bottom. And the same holds true
for the mind. I have to gear my mind up,
work it up in stages, the same way I do my
body."

*But surely you can remember the plays
from one season to the next.*

"I still know what's going on, but it's a
question of speed. When I start each season, my mind isn't used to moving the way
it does playing football. I've been doing
some other things, using my head in different ways, and when we start working in
the summer I have to begin pulling my

mind together for the job at hand. The first
or second game in the summer especially,
my mind is moving a little slow. I go up to
the line and I see something but I'm not
really sure about it. It looks like there's
something there I could take but nuts, the
play I've already called in the huddle still
looks pretty good and I just let it slide, go
on with the play I've got called. Why stick
my fool head out? I'm not going strong,
having confidence in what I see."

*How do you want to be functioning?*

"The goal is to get my mind geared up
to where everything just goes click-click-
click. Wait a minute, something's moving
differently out there. Boom! Jump on it.
Change the play to get the percentages the
most in my favor."

*And it takes time to get this speed of
thought?*

"I usually need about five or six weeks
of practice and about four games before I've
got my mind going at the speed I want. It's
a good feeling then. You're moving, getting
after something the way you're supposed
to, taking the defense apart where it's
weak. It's all right to relax some off the
field, but on Sunday everything has to be
quick. Your throw has to be quick and your
mind has to be quick. If you're too relaxed
and lackadaisical, you sort of ease into
things instead of jumping right on."

*So the goal is to actually increase the
speed of thinking?*

"I don't know if 'thinking' is really the
right word. You're not out there trying to

puzzle things out. You did that during the week. In a game it's all reaction. See it and do it. During the week you get yourself prepared. On Sunday you turn yourself loose."

*Do you ever have any problem doing enough work during the week to get ready?*

"Not against the good teams. They stay with you all week. But against the weaker teams, I've got to do some talking to myself."

*What do you talk about?*

"First I think about the end of the year. When you look at the records of the top teams there's usually only a half game or game separating them. Every game counts, every week counts the same. And then not even thinking about the championship, it's just such a bad feeling to lose. I mean I'm not crazy competitive, I don't mind losing so much when I'm shooting pool or playing basketball with my friends. But football, that's my *job*. That's the main thing. And losing feels terrible. Not just for me, but for everybody else on the team, players and coaches and everybody. And when I come home my friends are all down. I call up my family and they're upset. It's just a down scene, losing. It's pretty tough to enjoy yourself much during the week if you blew the game on Sunday. So when I think about this a little bit on Tuesday, I don't find much trouble getting down to the job at hand."

*We've been talking about the mental aspects of the sport, but football is a physical game, a game of full-speed collisions. What do you think of all the hitting?*

# "You learn how to be a gracious winner and an understanding loser."

"I don't like it. It hurts, you know, and I'm not into pain particularly. I'm not a masochist. The guys playing this game get bigger and quicker every year and talking about just watching the game, I love to see them play. I was really sorry Bubba Smith got hurt last hear because he's a good one, I enjoy watching him. But being out there on the field with those guys, that's rough. Us little dudes are always getting bent in half."

*You must find it hard to stay calm, stand in the pocket and throw the ball.*

"It's weird. It's not a natural feeling at all, just standing there trying to pay attention to what's going on forty yards away and meanwhile here's all these cats trying to crunch you. It's not an easy thing to handle. I have to gear up for that again every year, too."

*What do you do?*

"You get used to it. The first time you get knocked down, it's kind of a shock. But you get yourself back together and throw a few more, and then you get hit again. The second one is not as bad as the first. And by the time you've been knocked down twenty times and got up twenty times, what difference does the twenty-first make? Hell, they can have you then. You've got a job to do. It gets to where you almost don't notice what's happening to you. I've had guys come up to me after the game and say, 'Man, you took a couple of shots.' I don't remember getting hit. By the time I'm climbing up from going down I'm already thinking about the next play."

*Thinking about all the various experiences you have had playing football, do you think you have learned things that have helped you in your life as a whole?*

"I have. There's no doubt. If you want help keeping track of your ego, for instance, football will do it. It can be tough on you. It can be a humbling experience. More than humbling—downright humiliating. It'll keep your head in line, buddy."

*Even for someone who has had as much success as you have?*

"I've had six of my passes intercepted in one half. In one *half*. You're trying to keep your confidence up and here come six guys running your passes back at you. We get some nice things done out there, and it feels good to do it right, but there's not much chance to get an inflated opinion of yourself. You have to learn respect for the other guy because you may beat him on this play, but he's a pro, boy, and he's going to turn around and beat you on the next one. You learn how to be a gracious winner and an understanding loser. I appreciate what the game has done for my head."

*In terms of winning and losing?*

"Yeah, that, and also it does good things for being honest. I'm a pretty confident guy. I know what my abilities are. I know that if you add up all the things a quarterback needs—the ability to throw, to read defenses, to call plays, to lead the team—that nobody has ever played the position any better than I do. But there's no

# "I even talk to trees a little, say, 'How you doing?' They're a part of life."

way I can try to say I'm the son of super-man. I find out differently every Sunday.

"I'm a religious guy, too, and that has something to do with this. I don't mean I'm religious like some people where they are steady church goers and they don't cuss and so on, but as far as believing in God and that he is responsible for everything, I'm a firm believer in that. He's there and he knows and the thing is I know I can't cheat him. I can't get big-headed about any-thing because if I do I get embarrassed about it."

*Thinking that way ought to keep your pride down.*

"Yeah, it helps. You know, the basics of life are really pretty simple, at least the basics of my life. It's simple to do things right, not to cheat or to lie, not to be rude to somebody and hurt them. Your mind isn't troubled five minutes later, ten min-utes later, years later. You don't have to look back and say, 'How could I do that?' We're all in this thing together, you know, all the people, all the animals even, and the plants, too. It's got to be easier on the mind if we don't deliberately give each other trouble."

*You even think about plants this way?*

"Sure. They're a part of life and we're a part of life. Sometimes I even talk to trees a little, say, 'Hey, how you doing?' Maybe it doesn't seem like they are communicating with me, but at least I can try to communi-cate with them, tell them I feel good about them. I guess it's just a feeling that's natu-

ral to me. The thing I like best about foot-ball, for instance, is working as a group, the association with the guys on the team."

*Vince Lombardi used to say the players on a football team have to love one another.*

# "If you don't like to worry, why do it? It doesn't help your performance."

"I don't know if love is the right word, but the idea is good. You're in there fighting together, and you look out for each other. You take care of each other. But I don't know if that means you love each other. It depends on how you generally use the word. I don't usually say that I *love* John Riggins."

*What would you call it then?*

"I'm not sure. It's a complicated situation. A team feeling is not just a rah-rah, superficial kind of thing. You go through a lot together, working hard and winning some and losing some, and you get pretty tight. And it's not that easy working together. Especially at quarterback it can get to be a problem as far as play calling and leadership go."

*How do you mean?*

"We'll be out there in the huddle and a receiver will say, 'I can beat this guy,' and somebody else on the line will say, 'Just run it over here, Joe,' and that can get to be a hassle sometimes. I mean, I want to hear what everybody has to say and I have confidence in everybody that they can do their jobs. But I'm the quarterback and I have to make decisions based on what is soundest at the moment. I don't want one of my teammates to think that I don't have confidence in what he can do, but still I can't go with what somebody wants if it's not the sound thing at the time. It's a tough kind of problem."

*Once a couple of years ago you were knocked down hard and your center, John*

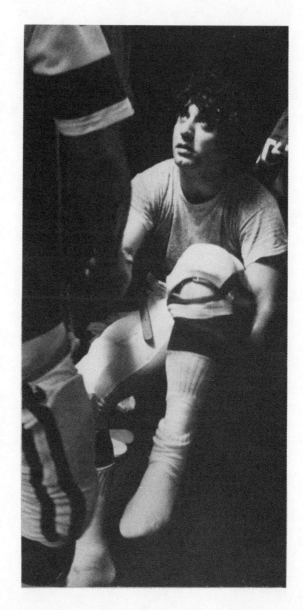

# "If I think about the image I have in public, I really wouldn't change anything."

80

*Schmidt, leaned over you for a long time and then helped you up and adjusted your helmet and snapped your chin strap up.*

"Yeah, I remember that. That's the way John is. He's concerned about all of his teammates."

*Does it embarrass you when somebody fusses over you like that in front of people?*

"No. I know what John is like. I appreciate his feelings. Sometimes I think linemen really understand football best. They're not in the limelight so they focus more on the game itself. And they know that it's all teamwork, helping each other out. It's a good feeling being part of something like that."

*Joe, one of the striking things about your career is the somewhat wild image the media has given you. In fact, you have said you no longer read the stories about you. Is it because they have distorted the truth about your life?*

"No, that's not it. Most of the things you have read about me, I've done things like that at one time or another. It's just that usually the stories you hear and the things I've done don't go together at the same time in the same places with the same people. But even if the various incidents people have heard about me are usually wrong, if I think about the image I have in public, I really wouldn't change anything."

*Do you ever deliberately play at being Joe Namath, the guy people have read about?*

"Sometimes I've done that. Maybe I'll meet some people in a bar and they'll start kidding around with me and I'll get into it and come on strong and have a good time. If people like you, if they want to laugh at you because you make them happy, well good. Make them laugh. Or sometimes I come on as Joe Namath because it can help me get a good seat at a club or something. You do that. I took my father to see Elvis Presley in Las Vegas once. My father was a big fan of Elvis. We got a good table and then afterward I asked him if he wanted to meet Elvis. He did, naturally, and so I just told the people to ask if Joe Namath could come backstage and my dad got to meet Elvis and they sat and talked for a long time. I think Elvis was great, a nice dude, and my father loved it, and that made me happy."

*That seems like a positive use of your image.*

"Yeah. If being Joe Namath can bring somebody pleasure for some part of time, well, then, I'm happy to do it."

# Don Maynard

"I try to set my goals up there real high,
and then be serious about reaching them."

# Don Maynard

**"In the long run, men hit only what they aim at. Therefore . . . they had better aim at something high."**

*—Thoreau*

**B**y the time Don Maynard retired, he had caught more passes than anybody ever, for more yards than anybody ever, and finished second only to Don Hutson in the number of times he concluded a pass play in the end zone. His final numbers— 663 receptions, 11,834 yards and 88 touchdowns—were a testimony both to his skill and to fifteen years of determination (a testimony untainted by the fact that Charley Taylor later broke the total receptions record).

Maynard is a wiry, plain-spoken Texan, a range-hand type who transmuted the Western independence and self-reliance of yesteryear into the drive and prickly pride that made him an All-Pro. He was cut after his first year with the New York Giants (1958: he played briefly in the famous sudden death championship with the Baltimore Colts), but he didn't quit. He played a year in Canada, then caught on with a new American Football League team, a Houston franchise that ended up in New York with Joe Namath as quarterback. Bombs soon filled the sky in previously undreamt proportions and Maynard ran under them and into the record books.

He accomplished all this despite high school size (170 pounds) and deceptively slow cuts. Don Maynard made himself great. When you ask him how he did it, his forthright answers might gladden the heart of any fan of the Triangle of Success. A proponent of that three-pointed theory might sum up Maynard's discussion like this:

1.  Strong Thought: his mental toughness and high standards of excellence
2.  Dynamic Action: his willingness to work hard to meet his standards
3.  Honest Assessment: his commitment to self-evaluation through inter-personal honesty

In any conversation with Maynard, however, such as this one from 1973, his ideas emerge simply as the best of Texas talking, as natural expressions of the self-reliance bred on those boundless, spreading plains. At the time of this talk Maynard was coming off the year in which he broke Raymond Berry's career reception record.

"It's getting tougher, though," he said. "Seems like every season it gets a little harder to catch the passes."

*That's understandable. You're going to be 36 this season.*

"That's not the problem. My legs feel fine and I feel like last season was one of my best in a while. It's just that the defenses are getting tougher. You take the Oakland game on Monday night last year.

# "You get the attitude that you want to be a winner. Then you train for it."

I caught seven passes and broke Berry's record, but none of that came easy."

*What was the difficulty?*

"They're playing good pass defense. A lot of times they have five backs in the game, five fast guys to cover three receivers. And they keep changing up their coverages."

*What do you have to do to beat them?*

"You have to be real alert. Say I'm going to run twenty yards and break to the inside. As I run down the field, I've got to feel where the linebacker is in there behind me while I'm driving that cornerback deep in front of me. When I break in, I can't let the linebacker wind up standing between me and the quarterback. I have to know whether to break in hard, or just turn in and stop. Namath is looking at the same people and in a way he's got an easier job. He just throws the ball into the hole in the defense, where the linebackers aren't. He throws while my back is still turned and then I make my break depending on where I think the hole is. When I turn around, the ball's there. We both have to read the defense right. It takes some practice."

*What else is there to it from your end?*

"Catching the ball. There's no use getting open if you don't want to catch the ball. I've only dropped one pass in two years. That was last year against Houston. I had been hit in the left arm and it was sort of paralyzed. I reached out for a perfect long pass and was getting ahold of it with my right hand when a safety hit me a good lick. It all happened pretty much at the same time and I dropped the ball. The coaches didn't call it a drop, but I did and that's the way I'll keep it."

*You have a good excuse for that drop. Why do you want to judge yourself so harshly?*

"It's the old story. You might be able to fool your coaches, or your teammates, or your opponents. But you can never fool yourself in anything. And I just believe that the more critical you are of your own performance—the higher the standards you have—the better you become at what you do. So I try to set my goals up there real high, and then be serious about reaching them."

*But how can you expect to catch the ball with only one arm?*

"Yeah, that arm was just sort of hanging there. I couldn't even do a push-up for fifteen weeks after that. But on that play I had the ball in my hands, and I didn't hold onto it. That's the story."

*Most receivers drop the ball sometimes. How can you prevent it?*

"I've always thought that success in football is about 10% physical and 90% mental attitude. I've got it in my mind that I'm going to catch the ball. I concentrate on it, get both hands on it, and when I do get ahold of it I *keep* both hands on it. Most times I'm fixing to get hit in the first five yards after the catch so I want to make sure I have a heck of a grip on the ball. Here again, I've only fumbled once in my whole

career—and I was fortunate that Pete Lammons recovered that one for us."

*And you believe mental attitude is the basis for performance like this?*

"The right attitude is the key to everything in the world. That and how you connect that attitude to the real world. If you want to be a winner, then you get the attitude that you want to be a winner. And then you train for it. The longer I've gone on in my career, the older I've gotten, the harder I've worked. I do more running, I do more stretching. In the last four years, I

haven't even missed one team workout. Not one. As you get older, maybe you get a half step slower, so you try to do anything you can to make it up, to make good. Whatever the price, I'm willing to pay it."

*Do you have any special pass receiving drills?*

"I play a lot of catch, and I have people throw me the ball high and low, left and right. And then there's something I got into a few years ago—playing catch with one eye closed. That makes you lose depth perception. You put your hands up for the

# "When you begin to accept your own weaknesses, that's when you're a man."

ball and just keep looking and waiting and it seems like the ball takes forever to get to you. It helps concentration."

*You and Namath have worked together a long time now. That has to help. You must know each other pretty well by now.*

"Yeah, we do. We've got one pattern, a quick out, that he can throw blindfolded. He really can. We tried it one day and hit four out of five and the fifth one I just did touch. It's like you can put your finger up and touch your ear even though you can't see it. He can throw me a quick out without looking."

*How do you get along personally?*

"I think Joe and I have a good friendship, as good an understanding as anything going. We can talk together and if there's anything bothering us, we can get it out in a couple of minutes where others might take all day to get around to it. We got a fast start on this kind of relationship. Right from the first when we'd miss on a pass we'd get back and discuss it right away. We didn't want to carry bad feelings around even for two or three plays. What happened? Was I early or were you late or what? And we got it right, got to where we could talk to each other. And we told each other, 'Let's get together. I'll help make you famous and you help make me famous.' "

*It sounds like you are pretty tight. Why do you suppose more people can't talk to each other like you two can?*

"People carry things inside them they don't want to discuss. They hide their feel-

ings if they think it will be unpleasant to talk about them. Maybe it comes from not having anybody to talk the truth with when they're growing up. But most folks, like guys on a football team, if somebody is doing something to them, kidding them or riding them, usually the guy who is getting kidded won't say his feelings out. He won't take the other guy aside and tell him he doesn't like what's going on."

*That's hard to do, though. It's an uncomfortable feeling to tell somebody you don't like what he is doing.*

"Maybe, but I think you should go ahead and talk anyway. Respect each other. I think that people basically want to do things to make other people happy, if they know what those things are. Even if they disagree, they'll help each other out if they can communicate. And if somebody has some special problem, I think he ought to be told about it. A lot of times people don't know what their own weak points are. But it's like my dad told me, 'When you begin to accept your own weaknesses, that's when you're a man.' Because that's when you can begin to do something about them. And I think you can learn about your problems faster if you have some help than if you try to find out everything on your own. Joe helped me learn to run patterns better. And I hope I can help other people. If somebody has bad breath, I'm going to tell them. And I hope somebody would tell me."

*Outside of such personal realms, what weak points do you have?*

# "What is old, anyway? J. C. Penney started his business when he was fifty-nine."

"Talking football, my weakest point is blocking. I know that and accept it, even though I feel like I had my best year blocking last year."

*What caused the improvement?*

"I changed my shoulder pads and got a little more protection. And then there might have been a little note in my contract about a bonus for blocking."

*Do you like to block?*

"It's a good feeling. In that Oakland game on national television I got a key block on the only guy who could have caught Richard Caster on a touchdown. And I heard that the block was on instant replay a couple of times. That feels good. All year I think I got in the way of people pretty well."

*Got in the way?*

"Well, I don't hurt anybody blocking. Not at my size. My blocks are more like basketball screens. I just try to get in the way, make the guy break stride to where he can't make the play. If you do that, it's considered doing your job."

*You have already played longer than any receiver in football's history. How much longer do you think you'll go on?*

"I'll tell you, the older I get, the more I want to play. Ever since they first handed me a check for playing football, I knew I was onto a good thing. I won't go quietly."

*A lot of players seem to want to quit when they are on top, while they are at their peak.*

"How do you know when you've reached your peak? I feel like I'm getting better all the time. I'm not dropping the ball, I'm staying free of injury, and I'm getting smarter all the time. This is what I meant: if you have the right attitude, you just keep on winning. What is old, anyway? J. C. Penney started his business when he was fifty-nine. It's amazing what guys can do, or what they *could* do, if they would just have the right attitude."

*So it's back to attitude. But don't you think it's easier for some people than others? Don't you think some people have more problems than others to overcome?*

"This is what I believe. The Lord made us all winners. He didn't put us here to be losers. Success is there for everybody, in some field. We just have to go out there and do it."

*But what about the problems?*

"You know the story about Norman Vincent Peale? Some guy was complaining to him about all his problems, just going on and on. So finally Peale took him in his car. He drove him out to a cemetery. He stopped the car and pointed out the window at all the gravestones and he said, 'Now there's a bunch of people with no problems.' And that's what I'm saying. There are challenges everywhere in life, on the football field and off. But we can lick them."

*Success is for everybody?*

"I firmly believe that. The world *does* owe us a living. The only thing is this: we have to go out and collect."

# Willie Lanier

"You will do best if you get back to the sandlot attitude and try to score because it's fun."

# Willie Lanier

**"He that wrestles with us strengthens our nerves and sharpens our skill. Our antagonist is our helper."**

*—Burke*

Willie Lanier is a model citizen/athlete In 1972 he won the NFL Man of the Year award, an award for people superlative on and off the field. It was due recognition for one of the greatest linebackers and one of the finest gentlemen ever to play the game. As a player, Lanier earned wide public recognition for his aggressive tackling in the middle of the Kansas City Chief defense. But teammates and coaches were as impressed with his wide-ranging and intelligent pass defense. In his eleven-year career, 1967–77, Lanier intercepted twenty-seven passes.

Athletic talent is only part of the Lanier story, moreover. He is one of the brightest people in the game, and from early in his career was distinguished by the thoughtful, philosophical approach he took to the sport. He played hard, but a strong thought process was evident in every action he took. He didn't back off from competition, but he didn't let it consume him, either. His attitude applies to anyone in any field, and it might be summed up in a few words: How good can you be while remaining fully human? This interview, including its brief introduction, was written in 1973.

The Kansas City Chiefs present a large number of unpleasant problems for their weekly opponents, and among these portable disasters none happens to the hapless victims more often than Willie Lanier, the multi-talented middle linebacker. Lanier is an imposing personality, confident and commanding. He is also one of the great hitters, and for this reason it is amazing to hear him make an unusual admission.

"I don't hit as hard as I can on every play," Lanier says.

*Willie Lanier doesn't hit hard?*

"Not all the time. Sometimes I can see that the way a play is shaping up, the percentages are that I will get hurt if I make a big hit. If that's the case, I won't do it."

*Are you afraid of getting hurt?*

"I play with the safety factor in mind."

*It's rare to hear a football player say that he plays carefully.*

"You can't play recklessly in this league. You can't annihilate these people. Everybody is as big as you are. They're all good athletes. Over a period of time, if you attack everyone all-out, you wind up doing more damage to yourself than to anybody else. I tried to do it that way my first year, but one play taught me my lesson. Now I get several good hits in every game—but I select the hits. I make sure everything is set up the way I want it. If I'm off-balance, or at a bad angle, I just make the play without excessive force."

*Aren't you afraid that other athletes will lose respect for you if they know this?*

## "I look around and I have to ask, Who hits like I do?"

# "I enjoy the concept of matching my body against another man."

"The way I play this game, it will never be noticed. I look around the league and I have to ask: Who hits like I do? My style is of such an aggressive nature that if I slack off sometimes, I'm back to what everybody else is doing normally."

*But even if this style doesn't show, doesn't it still leave you physically vulnerable? One of football's oldest sayings is that injuries happen when you start to be careful.*

"Yes, we've heard that a lot, haven't we? But I have to ask: Who says that? Who keeps that in circulation? I don't know who thinks that it is bad, or injurious, to be careful. I'm a professional. I have a wife and family. I have to be concerned with my well-being. And I know that if I play recklessly on every play, I'm exposing myself to serious injury. You see, I've been there."

*You mentioned one play that happened to you when you were a rookie.*

"That was the time. I attacked somebody head first, and I took the punishment. I was out cold on the field. I spent a week at Mayo Clinic being tested and a lot longer worrying if I would really be right again. I've been there. And if I can control it, I'm not ever going to be there again. I'm not going to simply throw my body into the action in any shape or form. I'm not going to take a chance on a fractured neck. There's no way I'll ever try to hit anybody head on again."

*That goes against another football saying—that good hitters stick their head in.*

"And again I ask: Who said that?"

*You wear an unusual helmet. Does that stem from your head injury?*

"It does. It's really a standard helmet, but it has extra rubber padding on the outside. I don't really know if it has any technological merit, if it really disseminates the shock. It's basically a psychological thing, to remind me not to use my head for tackling at all."

*You almost sound as though you don't really like contact, that you just put up with it.*

"No, I've always enjoyed contact a great deal. A good hit is beautiful. I enjoy it. But that doesn't mean I'm going to risk

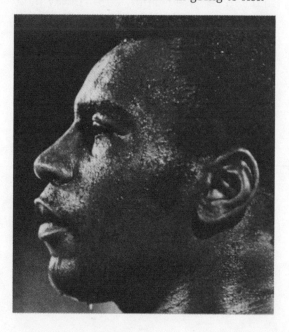

# "If you let the pressure of winning get to you, it can tie you up."

my life. Nor will I become an animal. Trying to hurt someone doesn't turn me on. Taking a swing at somebody near the sidelines isn't my bag. But I've always loved the clean hitting. As a matter of fact, I was just back home looking at some films of myself playing in high school. I wanted to see if I've changed my style of play much. I really haven't."

*What is there about the contact that attracts you?*

"I enjoy the concept of competing, of matching my body against another man. I respect my opponent. It's like two boxers. They can go at each other for ten rounds and still be friends afterwards—throw their arms around each other and say, 'You're a hell of a man.' When I was a boy my brother and I used to go at each other. We'd always get on opposite teams in the make-up games just to add a little spice to the contest. But when it was over we were still brothers."

*You say that you enjoy competing. But do you enjoy it when you lose?*

"I'll answer that this way. You know the playoff game we played at Miami—that long, long game? We lost that game but I believe that was one of the most enjoyable games I ever played, from a competitive standpoint. Playing the game is what is important. I try to remove the pressure of winning from my mind and just see how my skills stack up against the other players. Pure competition."

*Do you think that a professional football team could play well if it paid less attention to winning and more to playing?*

"Definitely. I feel that if you have a good squad, you will do best if you stress involvement in the game rather than the final result. Get back to the sandlot attitude, where you're trying to score points because it's fun. If you let the pressure of winning get to you, it can tie you up. If you start worrying about the Super Bowl, TV, sportswriters, fans—it can all weigh on you. You become too afraid of making mistakes. You aren't free to play your best. You get away from the basics of human nature; you are human, and it is human to err."

*Perhaps this all sums up quickly: football is a game, not a war.*

"That's correct. You have to keep your perspective. I got a lot of recognition last year. I was all this and all that. I enjoyed it. But what does it really mean? I was successful as a football player, but how important is that when you compare it to a space shot? Or compare it to the President trying to make his wage-price policy work? You have to be realistic. Basically, all I do is entertain people."

*The fans, of course, enjoy big hits.*

"So do I. So do I."

Russ Francis

# Russ Francis

**"The main thing is consistency. It's no good to just make a big play now and then."**

**"The better part of one's life consists of its friendships."**

—*Lincoln*

**R**uss Francis is an outrageous athlete. He stands 6'6" tall. He weighs 245 pounds. He is the fastest man on the New England Patriot squad. And he jumps off hotel balconies into tiny swimming pools far below. Russ is from Hawaii, where he learned how to have a good time, and he hasn't forgotten how in his five pro years; occasional motorcycle wipe-outs have been known to cost him Pro Bowl appearances.

Not much else can keep him out of that game, however. He is the walking definition of a tight end: big and mean enough to bull the linebackers, and fast and cute enough to dust the deep backs. And when Francis catches the ball and turns upfield looking for people to run over, its a sight for which parental discretion is advised.

With all this talent overflowing in every direction, it's surprising that Russ Francis' main focus in this interview is on the people who have helped him. What he talks about at length are the coaches who have advised him. Even gargantuan genius, it seems, can use some friendly feedback. In Francis' case, moreover, it's clear that "external" assessment has increased his own "internal" assessment. A view from the outside can improve the view from the inside.

In the course of the interview, Francis also gives his angle on the rewarding experience of teamwork and discusses the avocation common to many champions— self-competition. The discussion starts, however, in typical Francis fashion, with his tongue firmly in cheek and certain parts of his truth smuggled in as light banter. You ask him for his biggest football thrill, for instance, and he answers,

"Survival. Just survival."

*Just getting by?*

"There are some big people pounding on you, you know. A guy could get hurt."

*Then why are you out there?*

"You're trying to get me to think about this seriously?"

*If it's all the same.*

"Well, then, there are a lot of reasons I like pro football. And one comes to mind right away. I like to compete against myself."

*Football is much more complex than, say, running a mile. How do you compete against yourself with all those people around you?*

"The main thing is to generate consistency. To make my blocks consistently, to catch the ball consistently. It's no good to just make a big play now and then."

*Is consistency difficult?*

"You have to pay attention to it. Say I want to run a certain pass pattern, a cross over the middle. I'm supposed to be out there a certain number of yards at a certain time. But first I've got to get past a defen-

# "I enjoy everything about pro football a lot better than I thought I would."

sive end charging into me and a linebacker who wants to knock off my head. Sometimes the safety takes a shot at me."

*So you are competing against others.*

"Yes, but the main challenge is within myself. I'm supposed to be good enough to get past all that and make my break just right. And I'm supposed to get it up and do it right every time. Consistency. Staying with it is the main thing."

*What happens if you don't get out to the break on time?*

"The quarterback looks bad."

*The quarterback?*

"That's it. A lot of times you'll see a pass go whistling off into empty space. Now the fans may think the quarterback is having a bad day when really I just didn't run my pattern. The ball was there. I wasn't."

*And you enjoy the chance to keep improving your performance?*

"I do. In fact, I enjoy everything about pro football a lot better than I thought I would."

*You weren't the kind of kid who dreams about making it in the pros?*

"You have to realize I'm from Hawaii. I didn't figure I'd ever be doing *anything* in New England in the winter, let alone playing pro football. In the 1960s they didn't have any satellite television, so Hawaii didn't have any pro games on TV. We were all out surfing on Sundays. The first professional game I ever saw, I played in. So I think you can say that pro football was never high on my priority list."

*That's changed now, obviously.*

"It has, and I think the main reason has been the other players and the coaches—the people who have touched my life and made a significant impact."

*Who stands out?*

"Two men, really, the two coaches who have worked directly with me, the receiver coaches, Ray Perkins and Ray Berry."

*What contribution have they made?*

# "It made me think. I had to take stock of myself and make some decisions."

"Take Perkins. He's an excellent coach. He's the head man with the Giants now. He taught me a tremendous amount about football and a lot about life in general. Off the field he's one of the most jovial people I know, and he's a real friend. Anytime I had a problem, Ray was the first man I'd go to. On the other hand, when it came to football, the best word for Ray Perkins was *intense*."

*Why "on the other hand"?*

"This is what Ray Perkins is like. I broke my nose in a playoff game against Oakland in my second year. We went in at halftime, my nose was off to one side of my face, blood was everywhere. Perkins came up to me and said, 'Can you play?' I said, 'Gee, coach, I'm in a lot of pain.' He said, 'Can you play?' I said, 'I don't think I can.' And he just turned and walked away."

*How did that make you feel?*

"It made me think. I had to take stock of myself. I had some decisions to make."

*Weren't you upset with him for being so cold?*

"He didn't put a lot of pressure on me. He didn't call me an idiot or anything. He just went off to coach his football team. And I knew Ray. If I had something serious he wouldn't let me out there. This was just a broken nose, you know, not a broken neck. The question was the pain."

*What did you decide?*

"I played."

*Why?*

"After Perkins walked away, I just sat there and looked around the room. I saw a lot of guys who I knew were playing hurt. And I think it was right there that I finally realized pro football is really important to me. Being here had just sort of happened, you know, but I realized then that I was part of something that made a big difference to me. I was part of a group of men who were willing to make tremendous sacrifices for each other in order to reach a common goal. That's a rare experience."

*You think so?*

"I do. I think most of the time, in business, say, people come together because they *want* something from each other. On a football team you have forty-five guys who are there *giving* everything they've got. There's respect involved. There's understanding involved. There's love involved. It's a rare experience in any day and age."

*This is pro football, of course. Money makes a difference.*

"I like money. Most of us are fond of it. But I wasn't going out there with a broken nose to earn my check that week. In the first place, I'd get the check anyway. I don't care what people say, whether they think its money, or ego, or a macho thing—to prove that you're a man. No matter how corny it sounds, you go out there for your teammates. Your team is trying to win. It takes everybody who can make it. You know your buddies would get out there if they could. And you play."

# "No matter how corny it sounds, you go out there for your teammates."

*So you think you made the sensible decision?*

"If you talk to me *now* about playing with a broken nose, bleeding, so much pain I can't see, I'd tell you you're out of your mind. I've got more sense than that. But that's what happens when you play around people like Ray Perkins. You find more in yourself than you knew you had."

*What effect has Ray Berry had on you? He had a great career as a receiver with Johnny Unitas and the Baltimore Colts. Does he talk to you a lot, trying to pass on information?*

"Actually, no. He hardly ever says anything."

*Then how does he coach you?*

"I'll tell you the day I figured Ray Berry out. I had had a sprained wrist. It was real cold for days, and hard to run. Put it all together, I wasn't getting to practice much. Then, out of the corner of my eye at one workout I see Ray Berry toss the ball to me. I catch it. I throw it back. It's his ball after all. He throws me another one, and I get the picture he wants to play catch. So we start to throw the ball back and forth. He's just smiling. I find myself watching Ray Berry catch the ball, and it's exciting. It's easy to see why he was so great. He watches every ball in, tucks it away. He's so precise. And there I am learning how to catch the ball."

*Without talking.*

"He hardly said a word. Never said, 'You haven't been catching well.' Never said, 'Look at me, I'm great.' We just played catch. Now and then he'd say, 'Eyes,' or 'Tuck it,' one or two words. But the message gets across. You begin to think about yourself, how well you've been doing. You start to concentrate more without even trying. Since then we've played a lot of catch. By now if somebody throws

# "We're assembled together to achieve the impossible in an atmosphere of insanity."

102

me a *pencil*, I look it in and tuck it away."

*How else does he help you?*

"He's amazing. He's a Professor Emeritus in football, a Ph.D. in the passing game. And he always wants to know the fine points of what is going on in your mind."

*What do you mean?*

"Maybe we're watching films of Sunday's game. Say I got lit up on a certain play—really hit good. He'll say, 'What were you thinking about after that?' I'll say, 'Pain. I was thinking pain.' He'll say, 'How did that affect you on the next play?' "

*Why does he ask that?*

"He's making sure of your self-awareness. He doesn't want you out there like a zombie. He wants you thinking, being alive to your situation. If you know what's going on—in the game and in your head—you can react, adjust, change things. He doesn't want you trapped by lack of awareness."

*He sounds like a Zen coach.*

"Yeah, the cosmic coach from Kalamazoo. I saw a pamphlet the other day written by Maharishi Mahesh Yogi. Well, guys like Berry and Perkins, they're my Maharishi. I wasn't looking for it, but they've made a big difference in my life."

*And these are the experiences that mean the most to you as a football player?*

"Working with the coaches, yes, and like I said, being with all the players, too. It's a wild group. We've got sharecroppers from Mississippi, coal miners from Penn-sylvania and surfers from Hawaii. It's a fascinating group, a great group of men. And it's like I've told a lot of people: we're assembled together to try to achieve the impossible in an atmosphere of insanity."

*Most football players enjoy that team feeling a great deal. Can you explain why it means so much to you?*

"It's hard to put it in words. It's just so rich, so rewarding. Sometimes I'll be back home in the surf, out riding my board. I'll be sitting on it and thinking about all the funny things that go on in the locker room. A lot of times I'll just break up laughing, and guys in the water with me probably think I'm crazy. But what can I tell them? They don't want to hear about the time Steve Nelson put Stick-um in somebody's hair cream jar. It doesn't translate. But that unity, that closeness, it's a wonderful feeling. I'm sure of this. Never again in life will I get the experience of forty-five men giving all they've got for a common goal."

*The rest of your life should be pretty good, of course. You have Hawaii to go back to.*

"Yeah, but I'm going to miss this sport. I never thought I would, but I'm really going to miss it."

# Dan Fouts

**"If I don't get the ball to the right guy, I'm failing—and I don't like to fail."**

# Dan Fouts

**"They can conquer who believe they can."**
*—Virgil*

In 1979 Dan Fouts made it big. In his seventh pro year the San Diego quarterback went to the top of his profession, setting NFL records with 4,082 yards passing for the season and 300-plus aerial yards in four consecutive games. Though he led the League in number of attempts, 530, he also led in completion percentage, 62.6, an unusual double. On the whole, it's easier to complete passes if you don't throw them very often. On one memorable day against Seattle he threw thirty-five balls and completed twenty-eight, an astounding 80 per cent average. For his labors, Fouts was named All-Pro and picked AFC Player of the Year.

For those who watch him, however, it is not only his passing proficiency that impresses. As much as what he does, it's what he doesn't do that seems most remarkable. And what he doesn't do is move around much before he throws. Fouts drops back, plants that back leg, and then hangs in unmoving like a sailor in a thundersquall lashed to the mast. The wild war over his body rages all around him, but Fouts stands unflinching, full attention far downfield. It's a triumph of concentration amidst chaos.

It's not surprising, then, to find in Fouts another athlete who emphasizes the mental component of competition. He makes his contribution to the discussion by breaking down the winner's psychology into four parts—study, attitude, concentration, and control—giving his own angle on each. In addition, he reveals some interesting tips on leadership, the extension of his own thought to the people around him. There is one thing that does seem to escape his attention, however. When you ask him what he thinks about all those defensive monsters who get paid to pound him, he says,

"I don't."

*You don't what?*

"I *don't* think about them. That's not my job. I've got the ball back there in the pocket. I'm supposed to throw it. Straight. *That's* my job."

*But how do you manage to wall those people out of your mind?*

"What it all is, is the desire to make the play successful. There's a lot of people involved, and we've worked a long time, and I just don't want to let everybody down. I hate to see all our work go to waste. It's a very personal thing, too. If I don't get the ball to the right guy, I'm failing—and I don't like to fail. Everybody else on my team is playing his heart out. I'm going to stand in there and make the play work."

*What do you have to do?*

"You have to find the man who's open. You have to look out there and read the defense, and find the guy they're leaving."

# "My career has shown me that in order to win, you must expect to win."

106

*Is somebody always open?*

"Let's put it this way. If you go through your whole progression of reads, and you still have the ball, you're in a lot of trouble."

*Your description seems to emphasize the mental aspects of the game. You seem to take the physical act of throwing for granted.*

"Well, I don't want to overrate my head or anything, but I do think that my mental abilities are far superior to my physical abilities. And I do think that for any quarterback—maybe for any athlete—the mind is more important than the body."

*What are the mental qualities needed?*

"Well, first there's the study involved. You have to know the other team backwards and forwards—what you can expect them to do, and what you can do to counter them. You can't be a success in any field unless you study up. It may take six hours a day and it may take ten—you do what you have to to learn the job."

*What else besides study?*

"There's the psychological aspect."

*What do you mean by that?*

"That's not so much what you *know* as what your *attitude* is. How you feel about the game. And my career has shown me that, in order to win, you must *expect* to win. It's the confidence factor. In fact, you might even call it an arrogance factor."

*Why arrogance?*

"A good team has the feeling that, 'This is *our* game.' They get very upset with the other team because that team is trying to take their game away from them. Even if they lose, they figure they just lost it themselves. *They* did it. The other team hardly figures in. It's an arrogant type of confidence, a real attitude of superiority."

*You have been on teams that didn't have that?*

"Hey, we lost eleven games in a row in 1975. We weren't feeling too arrogant then. But in the last half of 1978 we won seven of eight. Last year we won twelve games. When you run up numbers like that, you know you can do it. You may get ten points behind in some game, but you know it's no big deal. It's your game. You know you'll find a way to win, and so you find it. Attitude—it's intangible but it's very important."

*That sudden Charger turn-around occurred when Don Coryell arrived as coach. What is the best thing he has going for him?*

"I don't think the man has any ego at all."

*No ego? What do you mean?*

"Some guys let their egos get in the way. A lot of coaches tell you, 'This is the way *I* want it done. Do it *my* way or you're gone.' But if Coryell has an ego, it's just all wrapped up around winning. He wants to do the right thing to win, whatever it is. So he's open to new ideas, wherever they come from. Maybe an assistant has a good idea. Maybe I have one. 'Fine,' he'll say. 'Let's do it that way.' He will adapt his

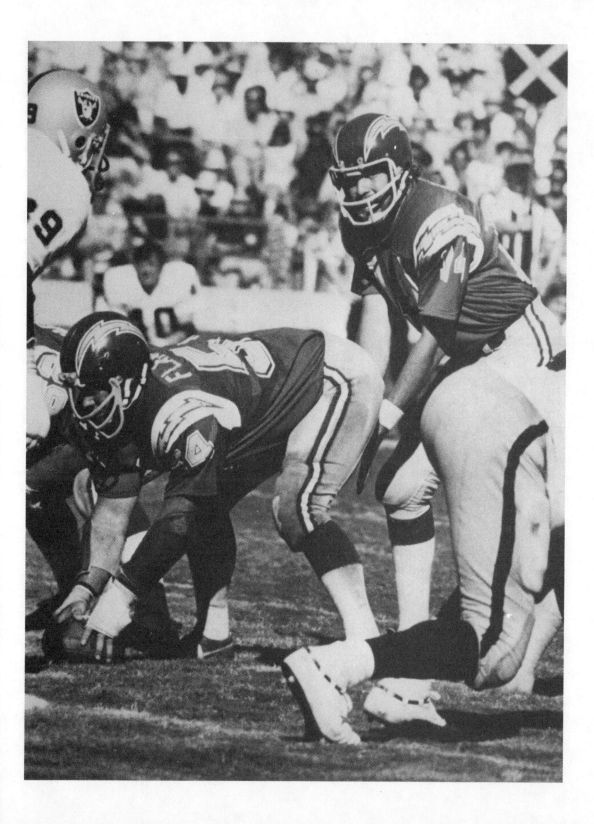

# "The key is to concentrate your way through the bad times."

109

approach to his players' abilities and his players' ideas. And he's not afraid to copy a successful play from another team. That's what I mean. His ego isn't in his way."

*He is known as a coach who loves to pass.*

"Yes, and that's mostly the confidence thing. A lot of coaches are afraid to pass."

*Don't many football people prefer to run the ball simply because it seems to them the more manly and courageous way to play?*

"That does figure in sometimes—the macho attitude. But a lot of it is just fear. Coaches emphasize the negative. They say that there's only three things can happen on a pass, and two of them are bad."

*But runners can get stopped for no gain, and they can fumble, too.*

"That's it. It's all in the attitude. The way Coryell looks at it, we average six or seven yards every time we try to pass. What running play can average that many yards? None. So the fastest way to move the ball is passing, and that's his bottom line: moving the ball and scoring points."

*We have talked about the need to study and about the importance of a confident attitude. What other mental factor is important to a winner?*

"Concentration. Concentration is all-important. You can't separate it from everything else you are doing."

*Do you think concentration difficult?*

"I think it's one of the toughest problems for a young quarterback. There are so many pressures and distractions in a game and throughout a season."

*What is the biggest challenge?*

"Maybe the moon and the stars. I'm no expert on biorhythms, but it's a proven fact that we all go through cycles. At some points you feel sharp and at others you don't. There are good times and bad times. And the key is to concentrate your way through the bad times."

*How do you do that?*

"I don't do anything too detailed. It's just that on a bad day, it's like a red light goes on in my head. It's a fail-safe mechanism. I realize I'm off and I know I better bear down harder or it's going to be a long afternoon. And I really believe that you can have some of your best games that way. You play better because you have to concentrate harder. It's like you'll see guys hurt all week who play great on Sunday. They get themselves going mentally because they know the body isn't all there."

*Is there anything else a winning quarterback needs?*

"One more thing is very important. You have to be able to control your emotions. The players look to what the quarterback is radiating. They see how the tide of the game affects you. So it's important to be careful what sort of feeling you are putting out."

*Do you find yourself ever having to fake it?*

"You don't *want* to put on a false face. But sometimes you have to. You just have

# "You don't want to put on a false face. But sometimes you have to."

110

to get up some bravado and psyche people up."

*Can you give an example of the type of emotional leadership a quarterback must demonstrate?*

"Well, let's say we've had a bad call by the refs. Now everybody is mad. The first thing is that the quarterback can't get lost in that. He has to stay on an even keel and give that anger some direction. The players are looking for a way to channel their aggression. You have to find one avenue, one pipeline, where they can let it all out."

*Is there ever a time when you want your emotions to show?*

"Sometimes. Usually the game itself provides enough emotion. If we play Pittsburgh, everybody is high enough already. I won't have to say a word the whole game. But say we're in against a last place team. They can still beat you. Anybody can beat you. That's when I may have to remind people, motivate them. I might holler a little more, get upset at people for making mistakes."

*Do you enjoy that part of your job?*

"I don't think I'd use that word. This is a very sensitive area."

*In what way?*

"Who am I to be screaming at these guys? These are professionals. They don't need some jerk hollering at them who never gets the seat of his pants dirty."

*But you do it anyway?*

"Sometimes. It's part of the job. And on our team I feel it's taken the right way. I feel very good about the relationships we all have on our team. The guys know that anything I say isn't personal, that it's all just in the framework of the game, and that I don't go around harboring grudges."

*You're sure they know that?*

"I make sure they know. After the game I'll go over and apologize to a guy. I'll explain what was happening in me, make sure there are no hard feelings."

*That seems like a decent thing to do.*

"I suppose. But it's also the smart thing. I don't want my players mad at me. They're my bread and butter."

# Gene Upshaw

"We figure if we keep coming at them,
by that last quarter, man, they're ours."

# Gene Upshaw

**"The credit belongs to the man who is actually in the arena; whose face is marred with dust and sweat; who strives valiantly."**

*—Theodore Roosevelt*

**G**ene Upshaw is on the Board of Governors of California Community Colleges. This doubtless makes him seem more respectable and urbane to defensive backs whom he has recently stomped into the ground. Though polite and well-spoken, Upshaw has long been, in truth, the most shattering force playing offensive guard in the NFL. He and his linemate, tackle Art Shell, have made the left side of the Oakland Raider line famous for it's earth-moving power.

It's easy to sense Upshaw's power just by hearing him speak. However you want to analyze a winner—using the tri-partite breakdown, strength of mind, energy of action and candor of self-estimation, or some other system altogether—Upshaw makes an ideal test. His strengths are readily apparent from even a casual conversation, and any theory of winning should look good after listening to him. With Gene Upshaw, what you hear is what you get.

There is one play that sums him up better than most. Gene Upshaw has become a virtuoso at one of the toughest assignments in football: leading a sweep. He is the left guard, and it's his job to get out in front of his running back on the left side excursions. It's a job that gives him a great sense of accomplishment, and it's easy to see why. There are few sights in football more fearsome than Gene Upshaw pulled wide and charging—careening top speed toward some hapless defensive back at the corner of the defense.

"That's my play," Upshaw says. "A wide receiver wants to catch a long touchdown pass. A defensive lineman wants to break in to sack the quarterback. I get my satisfaction pulling to lead those sweeps. That's a play where it comes down to just me and the defensive back. If I get him clean, we're going to make a long gain. If I miss him we don't get a yard."

*Aren't you worried about missing him?*

"It doesn't bother me at all. I'm coming at him weighing 260. He's 210 at most and 185 some of the time. And he hasn't got a chance. I've got it in my head that whatever he does has to be wrong. If he goes to the outside, I'm going to put him out of bounds. If he goes inside, I'll knock him in. And if he stands there man, I'm going right over the top of him."

*You really want to level those guys?*

"Yeah. Oh, yeah. I wind up on those dudes. See, I'm not only thinking about the sweep we're running right now. I'm thinking about the whole game. If I get out there and put it on that guy two or three times, I'm going to take something out of him. When it comes time for him to cover our wide receiver, he's going to be missing a step. Most of those guys aren't built to take a lot of punishment and I know I can slow

# "Running over those defensive backs is my biggest thrill in football."

115

them down. Running over those defensive backs is my biggest thrill in football and that's why I just love the sweep. If it was up to me we'd run it every play. I know football's a team game and I know I have to sacrifice and all, but I still wish we'd just sweep all day."

*What's the secret to a successful sweep?*

"The thing I think about most is getting out of my stance on the count going full speed. I run a 4.6 or 4.7 in the 40-yard dash, but the kind of backs we have, they do better than that. So I aim to get out of my stance quick and get a jump on them. Then they've got to stretch out to catch up with me and that means we're both going to be getting out to the corner in a hurry. And that's the main idea. There's nothing but trouble chasing us."

*When the Raiders aren't sweeping, their running game seems to be very basic. It seems to be mostly straight-ahead blocking.*

"Yeah, when a defensive lineman gets ready to play the Raiders he doesn't have to wonder what we are going to do. We're coming after him. We just pound at them play after play—power stuff in the first quarter and power stuff in the fourth quarter. We figure if we keep coming at them, by that last quarter, man, they're ours."

*Some pro teams use a high proportion of fancy blocking, plays where linemen pull the wrong way to fool the defense and other such tricks.*

"I know it. I can't believe it. We watch the films and it's amazing some of the garbage blocking these people get away with. That's not our style at all. Around here you block the man in front of you. And we don't even do much option blocking—taking the man whatever way he wants to go. On our running plays, we block the man where the coaches tell us to, or they get someone who can. It's basic stuff. It's just you and me."

*One of an offensive lineman's biggest responsibilities is pass blocking.*

"That's true. I don't have as much fun pass blocking, but I do get satisfaction from it. That's where we separate the men from the boys. It takes a hell of a man to stand in there on pass protection, to take those roundhouse clubs to the head and the butting with the helmets and all that. You've got to have control of yourself and be patient."

*Why do you have to be patient?*

"Because a good pass protection blocker sits and waits for the defense to make the move and then he reacts. You have to be passive and aggressive at the same time. If I lose my patience, if I get tired of getting clubbed all the time and decide I'm just going to charge and wipe the guy out, that's when I'm really going to be in trouble. If you charge too hard at some of these quick linemen, you'll get off balance and they'll just skip around you or grab you and throw you. Or worse yet, you could fire at your guy but the defense will be

# "People who think we've got a lark in this game, they've got to be nuts."

running a stunt and some other guy will come blowing right through the hole you left. You have to be patient. You have to sit back a little and wait for developments and then make your move."

*But if you are sitting back passively, how do you generate any power to block people?*

"That's the trick. When you do make your move on those guys, you have to pop out at them hard and stop their momentum. Otherwise they'll be heading right through for the quarterback and taking you with them. The thing is, if you're sitting back there in good football position, with your rear end down some, your feet spread and your weight balanced, when it's time to move you can really uncoil. You strike out at the guy, pop him in the chest with your helmet. He stops. Sometimes I think that pass protection is like being a boxer, kind of sliding around on your toes and being ready to deliver a blow when the time comes."

*Have you always been a good pass blocker?*

"We did a lot of pass blocking in college, at Texas A&I, and when I got to the pros I was all right as far as physical technique. But when I look back I still don't know how I got by in my rookie year. I didn't have any idea what was going on. I was just reacting as fast as I could. And this is where my biggest improvement has come, in reading the defensive guys and being able to tell what is going on. I'll spend a whole week looking at films now just to find one tip, one clue that will tell me what the guy in front of me is going to do."

*Why does it take a week just to find one tip?*

"Because these guys are smart. They're not going to show you anything if they can avoid it. In fact, sometimes they'll give you false leads. A tackle might line up leaning to the inside and then charge to the outside. Or the tackle and end may line up close together as if they were going to run a crossing stunt one behind the other, and then they just charge straight ahead. They make it tough on you."

*And you work all week to try to figure these things out beforehand?*

"That's right. People who think we've got a lark in this game, that all we do is go out and play a game on Sunday, they've got to be nuts. We put in three hours in class every day and two-and-a-half out on the field and after that you're really physically and mentally drained. You do that all week and go out and play on Sunday, and then the next week it's right back to work. A new team, a new set of problems."

*Are you sure it's worth the effort?*

"Oh, yeah. Just let me pull out and lead a couple of those sweeps and I'll be feeling fine."

# Gale Sayers

"Football is my game. No knee injury was going to keep me out of my game."

# Gale Sayers

**"The greater the obstacle, the more glory in overcoming."**

—*Molière*

ale Sayers did it as nobody has, before or since. He carried the ball in a full-speed crouch, and when it came time to cut he jammed one stiff leg heel-first into the turf and right-angled away like a ball off a wall. Often, in a crowd, both feet would come off the ground as he sailed forward in a moment of all-out pause; then whichever leg was needed would tip into the ground and he would be gone through a crack that only he could find. Like all great running backs, the Chicago Bear halfback was one of a kind. He was the best of his time, without doubt, and the best halfback in the NFL's first fifty years by vote of the Hall of Fame.

In mid-career, Sayers was felled by that most dreaded of all injuries for the running back: the knee. It was then that the sports world found Gale Sayers to be more than merely a gifted athlete. His injury was the disaster doctors know as the "Terrible Triad": three of the main ligaments were snapped. But if his physiology was torn apart, his mind was still strong and tightly knit. He had a clear idea of what he wanted to happen and he did what he had to do to make it happen. Sayers was back at the top of the running statistics the very next year.

A couple of years later Sayers hurt his knee again, and this time there wasn't enough left for the doctors to repair. But nothing could take away from the achievement of that first recovery. Speaking right after that comeback season, with a conviction that has a retrospective poignancy, Sayers said,

"Football is my game. I've been playing it for twenty years now. No knee injury was going to keep me out of my game."

*Weren't you afraid the injury would end your career?*

"I knew I'd be back. In fact, even before I was hurt, I had prepared myself. I decided that if I ever got a knee, I would come all the way back the very next year."

*But most ball carriers take two or three years to recover and some are really never the same.*

"I know that, and that was one of the reasons I wanted to come right back. Most runners are afraid of a knee injury. They've been brainwashed. They think it's supposed to take a long time to recover. I wanted to show them that it isn't so. I wanted to prove you could be ready by the next season."

*How can you overcome the physical fact of a weakened knee?*

"Most of the time, your knee *isn't* weakened. The doctors say that after they repair the knee joint, it is as strong or stronger than it used to be. You have to have faith in the doc. He does his job. Then you do yours."

*How did you start your job?*

"Four days after the operation, I walked out of the hospital without crutches. I never did use crutches in the six weeks I had the cast on. They're a nuisance. Besides, I figured it would help keep the muscles in my leg strong if I walked on it. I also lifted weights with the cast on— hung some weight on the end and did leg raises. It all paid off. Usually, after an operation like this, the thigh muscles atrophy two or three inches while the leg is in a cast. My leg only lost about a half inch."

*Then you were ready to start working out as soon as the cast came off.*

"Not exactly. When your leg comes out, it's frozen straight stiff like it was in the cast. A lot of adhesions have grown together in your knee where they aren't needed. You have to break the knee down before you can start to work with it."

*How did you do that?*

"With my hands. I got in the whirlpool every day, to loosen it up, then I'd grab it and try to bend it. It was three weeks and a lot of pain. Sometimes you can even hear the adhesions snapping. Some guys have to go back into the hospital and let the doctor break it down under sedation, but I wanted to do it myself. The more you can do to the knee without help, the less fear of it you'll have."

*How did you know when the leg was ready to lift weights?*

"As soon as I could bend it back to ninety degrees. Then I could sit with my

# "Most runners are afraid of a knee injury. They've been brainwashed."

121

leg over a bench and lift upwards until my foot was straight out in front of me."

*How much weight did you start with?*

"Five pounds, and after a knee operation and nine weeks of little activity, five pounds is agony. Lifting was the hardest part of the recovery. I did it three times a day, every day. I'd get up at five in the morning and go down to the basement and work. Then at mid-day I'd go to the gym, and in the evening I'd be back in the basement. I got up to sixty pounds and did 300 repetitions, thirty sets of ten. And everything I did with the bad leg, the right one, I did with the good one, too. It was hard work, and boring and lonely. The loneliness was the worst. After a week I was ready to say the hell with it. I'd tell myself that I'd do it tomorrow. But if you miss one day, it takes two to make it up, so I just stayed with it. I was going to come back and I was ready to pay the price."

*What else did you do besides lifting weights?*

"Well, at first when I would get done lifting in the gym, I'd go down to the swimming pool and kick up and back the length of the pool. Then, after about three weeks, I started to jog around the track. I was at that for about a month, when I started cutting some. Then I went to see the doctor. This was in February. He said the knee was ready."

*Did you believe him?*

"Yes, I did. I didn't stop working—as a matter of fact, I still lift weights now—but I knew the knee was well. I had lunch not long after that with Buddy Young and Emerson Boozer. Boozer was telling me I would have it tough. He said I'd be slow and have a lot of pain. I just told him I didn't think that's how it would be."

*Wasn't there ever a time when your knee got you down?*

# "You can come back.
# That's what I want everybody to know."

"Oh, yes, right after I was hurt it was pretty bad. But George Halas, the Bears' owner, helped me out of that. The doctor operated on me the day after I was hurt, on Monday, and when I came out of the anesthesia Tuesday, I was awfully low. I was worried about my contract. It was up for renewal that spring. But Mr. Halas came in to see me that afternoon and he told me not to worry about it—the injury would have nothing to do with my contract. That helped me a lot."

*I would think it would be depressing to hear so many people say you were through.*

"There was a lot of talk, all right. Reporters love to write about it. They say you'll be slow, you won't be able to cut. They always want to move you to flanker. But I just saw it as a challenge, and I like a challenge."

*Some people still don't think you are completely well.*

"I know it, and it irritates me. I led the league in rushing last year. I don't know what else I can do."

*Many of the athletes coming back from knee injuries would probably like to know how you taped your knee when the games started.*

"I didn't. I never put any tape on it at all. Tape isn't going to help if the knee isn't well. All it does is slow you down. I told the doctor just before he operated that I was never going to tape it."

*Did you have any trouble with the knee?*

"Not from the surgery. I got a completely new injury, a knee bruise, but the only time I felt the old injury was before I loosened up on cold days. Then it felt like somebody was jabbing me with ice picks. I think I can be a weatherman from now on."

*There would be one advantage to that occupation. You wouldn't be in a position to get another knee injury.*

"I know it, but I'm going to stick to football. It's my game. I know I could get hurt again. I carry the ball twenty or thirty times a game and there are eleven people keying on me. But I have the same attitude now that I did before the last injury. If I get another knee, I'll be back the next September."

*At least you've been through it once now. You know the tricks.*

"There aren't any tricks. It's hard work and pain and loneliness. But you can come back, that's what I want everybody to know. You can come back."

# George Blanda

"My job is to think about football.
I'm not over there on the sidelines day dreaming."

# George Blanda

**"I never did anything worth doing by accident, nor did any of my inventions come by accident; they came by work."**
—*Edison*

George Blanda was a survivor. He played an incredible twenty-six years of professional football, a career that spanned four different decades from the 1940s through the 1970s. He was outright cut twice, by the Baltimore Colts when he was only twenty-four and by the Chicago Bears when he was thirty-one. His best years were still ahead. He caught on with the Houston Oilers of the American Football League in 1960 and made league Player of the Year in 1961. He moved to Oakland in 1967 and became a national symbol of Grey Power, winning the AFC Most Valuable Player award in 1970 (after which this interview was written) at the age of forty-three. Among his monumental lifetime statistics are pro football records in the following categories (among others): most games played, 340; most points, 2002; most consecutive games played, 224; and (it goes with the package) most passes intercepted, 277.

Of all his football years, one shines brightest in the memory. George Blanda's 1970 season was a fable of our times. In his 21st professional year he went on a five-game mid-season streak that dominated sporting news across the country. Coming in usually in relief, he started by throwing three touchdowns against the Pittsburgh Steelers, then tied the Kansas City Chiefs with a 48-yard field goal in the last three seconds, drove for a late touchdown and then beat the Cleveland Browns with a 52-yard field goal in the last three seconds, drove to a touchdown to beat Denver in the last two minutes, and kicked a field goal to beat the San Diego Chargers in the last four seconds. It was a wonder of nature, as if a long dormant tree had suddenly blushed into full bloom.

Talking to him after that season, it was easy to understand his success. In the first place, George Blanda loved to play football. He enjoyed the endlessly unfolding puzzle that is pro football strategy, and he never stopped learning. In the second place, Blanda was powered by a powerfully combative spirit, a feisty, even crusty, essence that refused to go down. Like Floyd Little, he was a tireless battler who made desires into deeds and beat you from the inside out.

In that big season he was forty-three years old, six years older than the next oldest quarterback in the game, ten years past the normal retirement age. But when he was asked how he did it, his response summed him up.

"You know what my most difficult job was last year? It was answering that same question over and over. Every time we'd play a game, all these people would come over and ask me, 'How do you do it? Aren't

# "Of course I was tired. Football is a very strenuous game. It tires you out."

you tired?' Of course I was tired. Football is a very strenuous game. It tires you out. But what kind of news is that? Football fans want to know about the games—how you won or why you lost."

*But weren't you surprised to do so well at your age?*

"Why should I be surprised? I practice every day during the season. I know what I can do."

*Other athletes get to a certain point and then decide that they've reached the end. They get hurt too much or they can't do their job anymore.*

"I think most athletes quit simply because they lose their love for the game. I still enjoy it as much as ever. The only other thing that could knock a man out would be injuries and I've been fortunate there. I've only had one sore arm and my legs have been healthy now ever since a knee injury in 1946."

*After making so much news last fall, you had many dinners and award meetings to attend in the offseason. How did you feel about all that attention?*

"It was pretty tough to take. Every time I turned around somebody was after me for something. I was away from home all the time, running for airplanes, trying to make appointments. It was a tiring life."

*You don't like the life of a celebrity?*

"I'm not a celebrity. I'm a football player. I never thought about living like this before. But I guess I shouldn't complain. People have been good to me and it's opened

up some opportunities for me that I'll follow through on. Inside, however, I don't feel like a celebrity. This isn't going to change me inside. There were a lot of people who thought I was a pretty good quarterback before this, including me. We just had a dramatic season."

*It certainly was dramatic and amazingly successful, too. Taking 1970 in general, how do you feel about your performance?*

"It was a good year for the Raiders but it could have been better."

*I mean personally.*

"There isn't any personally in football. You are talking about either 'I' or 'we'. And football is a 'we' game."

*You were in there often last year in the last second or so and produced well. At some point you said this was because you didn't get excited any more.*

"No, I didn't say that. I was misquoted. Ninety-nine per cent of the time, when you are talking to people you get misquoted. Of course I get excited. This game is great fun. Standing in there and throwing the ball just before you get popped is a real thrill. What I said was something different—I said I don't get nervous any more."

*Why not?*

"What is there left for me to get nervous about? I've won games throwing and kicking, and I've lost games throwing and kicking. Everything has already happened."

*What about those games where you had to kick long field goals with only three seconds left? Didn't you feel pressure at all?*

# "Standing in there and throwing the ball before you get popped is a real thrill."

"My basic job with the Raiders is field goal kicker. That's what they hire me to do. When it's time to kick, I have to concentrate on the job at hand. I don't have time to think about the consequences or about people in the stands."

*What do you think about?*

"First, I have to zero in on the spot where the ball is supposed to be placed. Then I have to get ready in case the ball doesn't hit right on that spot. You can't always get a perfect hold. Then I think about the step, about locking my ankle, and about the arc of my swing. And besides my own actions, there's also the defense to remember. Against the Chiefs, for instance, when I had to kick one forty-eight yards, Buck Buchanan was down in the line waiting to rush me. He's 6'6" tall. So I decided to kick that ball higher to give him less chance to block it. These are the kinds of things that are going through my mind. If I get the ball up off the ground and headed in the right direction, I've got a chance. Nobody up in the stands can help me."

*Concentration like that must come from years of being a kicking specialist.*

"I don't think of myself as a specialist. Kicking the ball isn't really playing. You're out there a few seconds and you're a hero if you make a kick and a bum if you don't. I don't need that. I'm glad I became a good kicker because it has prolonged my career, but in my own mind I'm really a quarterback and if I thought I was never going to play again, I'd quit right now."

*Based on last season, you certainly will be playing some more quarterback. It always seemed you could move the team as soon as you came into the game. It looked like you knew what you wanted to do right away. If this is true, what accounts for it?*

"I'm supposed to know what I want to do. You'd be a hell of a reporter if you didn't know what to ask me, wouldn't you? Well, I'm a quarterback and I'm supposed to know what plays to call. That's a quarterback's biggest job. We have meetings all week, we watch hours of film to find the opponent's weaknesses. The coaches tell us what they want. Then I sit on the sidelines and observe, watching the defense for its strengths and weaknesses. When I go in the game, I just proceed to do what I know. My job is to think about football. I'm not over there on the sidelines daydreaming."

*It seems that you often throw a big pass to your tight end on your first play.*

"Not always. You don't do anything all the time. But that first pass should be a completion, to get the momentum going, and usually the tight end is the easiest guy to hit. He can usually find a slot in zone defenses. It's all according to the situation, though. You've got to call plays that will surprise the defense in its regular sets, and in its changeups, too."

*Are there any pass patterns you particularly like?*

"Actually, the pattern isn't as important as the pass. On any pattern at any

"I don't have time to think about consequences or about people in the stands."

# "Well, now, I'll tell you, football is a real simple game."

place on the field, the receiver is always open at some point. It's all up to the passer to have the ball at the right spot at the right instant with just the right amount of snap on it."

*Your plans are based partly on films and the coach's ideas. But do you have a basic philosophy of quarterbacking?*

"Well, now, I'll tell you, football is a real simple game. It's not nearly as complicated as people are led to believe. It all comes down to this—if the defense wants to give you something, you take it. You can't get greedy and try to grab something they don't want you to have. If you can run off tackle, why try to go around end? If they shut down the off tackle play, you have to probe around and find what they are leaving open. It's like checkers. You are always trying to stay one move ahead of the defense."

*You have been playing football for more than two decades now. Is it getting any harder for you to handle the defenses?*

"The defenses are more sophisticated now, but I don't think they confuse me. They don't upset me. You just have to keep on learning every year. There's no secret. You have to apply yourself and work at it. The defenses are getting cuter, but we're pros over on the offense, too, you know."

*There is a question whether you can physically perform another year at your age. How are you going to get in condition at age forty-four?*

"The same way I have the last couple of years. In the offseason I play handball several times a week. When the weather lets up, I do a lot of golfing, and when training camp gets near I begin to run four miles a day."

*What about throwing and kicking?*

"I never do any of that until I get to camp. I figure I could go out in the spring sometime when I wasn't ready and hurt myself. We've got nine weeks of camp to get into shape. When I first get there, I start out gradually and they usually let me set my own pace, but when I'm ready I take my full turn with the rest."

*How much longer do you think you can last?*

"As long as they want me. I'm in better shape now than I was a few years ago. The most important thing is whether you love the game, and I still do. Playing football is damn good fun."

# Floyd Little

## "He may be bigger than me, but his heart works the same way. He can go down."

# Floyd Little

**"I have learned this at least by experience: that if one advances in the direction of his dreams, and endeavors to live the life which he has imagined, he will meet with a success unexpected in common hours."**

—*Thoreau*

**T**hrough the late 1960s and most of the 70s, Floyd Little *was* the Denver Bronco franchise. Few men ever meant so much to their team. Anything that had to do with advancing the football, Little did. He is still the Broncos' all-time leading rusher, and he holds as well the first rank in kickoff returns, third in punt returns, fourth in pass receptions and first in total points scored. He is also one of the most popular men in Denver. A solid citizen and a successful businessman, he is a tireless booster of the joys of Colorado.

On the football field, the message of Floyd Little was that physical stature isn't as important as the size of the heart. Off the field, his whole life makes a similar point. Obstacles don't matter; it's desire that counts.

The parallels are instructive. In the game of football—as we have already seen with Jack Youngblood, Gale Sayers and others—the challenges of life often resolve simply to physical pain. But what happens when the simple, if painful, problems presented by bruises and broken bones are replaced by the more diffuse and perplexing problems of everyday life? Are excuses more sensible, failures more understandable? Not if we listen to Floyd Little. In his view, the same traits of thought and action that can get you off tackle can also get you through life. It's a point he begins by explaining, in this 1972 interview, his extraordinary longevity as a small pro ball running back.

"To keep going in this game," he says, "you've got to make a distinction between pain and injury. I wouldn't play more than one game a year—the first one—if I let pain keep me out. The trouble is, a lot of guys coming up now, they don't know the difference between hurting and being hurt."

*What's changed about the new athletes?*

"They're a different variety of people. They're tougher to deal with. And with a lot of them it shows up in the injury thing. They get a sprained wrist and they think they're not supposed to play. They get knocked out and they won't go back to play anymore. I don't know. I don't think that's what football is about. You've only got forty players on a team and you need them all. Hell, every time I run off tackle I may get a minor concussion. But if I can still remember the plays, I'm going to keep going."

*Have you played with any major injuries?*

"I've played with a broken clavicle, I've played with a broken back. I play hurt all the time. One thing I do have going for me

# "You've only got forty guys on a team, and you need all of them."

though. My body structure keeps me from getting many leg injuries."

*What's special about your body structure?*

"I'm bow-legged. I am the most bow-legged runner you ever saw. I'm the most bow-legged player who ever played the game. Some guy comes in and gives me a pop on the side of the leg and my knee just straightens up into a normal position instead of getting all ripped up."

*But you say you've played with broken bones. How do you do it?*

"That's just me. It kills me not to play. I had the broken transverse processes in my back the last two games in the 1970 season. The transverse process, that's a piece of the vertebrae where the muscles attach. I had so much pain I couldn't even get down in a three-point stance. But we put a lot of heat on it before the game and I played both those games into the third quarter. It's cold here in Denver in December and when the heat wore off I had to come out, but I played as long as I could. When I'm out there the defense still respects me even if I'm not going full speed, and that helps the rest of the offense. I do my job if I possibly can. It seems to me that's what football is about."

*Do you take shots to kill the pain of an injury before you play?*

"No, I don't believe in pain killers. I want to feel the pain. I want to know what's going on. Several times doctors have told me not to play but I tell them, 'If I feel

it hurt, I'll come out.' Like I said, you've got to know the difference between pain and injury."

*Not too many people who live normal lives will be able to understand your attitude. Most people spend their lives avoiding pain as best they can.*

"I know it. A lot of people tell me I'm stupid to play the way I do. Maybe so. All I know is I've only got so long to play football. I'm going to play every game I can, and I'm going to give it all I've got every time I play. When I get done I'm going to be able to say that I gave it hell while I was in it."

*Where did you get such a determined approach to what you are doing?*

"I've had to live my whole life this way. Think about when I came up to the pros. Everybody said I was too small. They still say it. Every time I go on the field, I've got to prove myself again. The same thing happened back in school. People said I'd never get into college. Then they said I'd never graduate. I've always been prejudged. I've had to fight for everything I got."

*Was there any one time that was a major turning point in your life?*

"Yes, there was. Right after I got out of high school. In school they had me on a program of shops and physical education. When I got through, I couldn't even read well. I was eighteen or nineteen and I was trying to get a job, but when I went to fill out job applications and answer questionnaires, I couldn't do it. All I was trying to

be was a custodian, a damn clean-up man, and I couldn't handle it. And I was smart enough to know that I wasn't failing to get the job because I was black. I was failing because I couldn't read the tests. I didn't know the terminology. I couldn't give any answers because I didn't understand the questions. I walked out of there knowing I'd never get the job, but I also knew that I was going to come back and make it."

*That's a tough trap—out of high school, undereducated. How did you get out of it?*

# "When I got to Syracuse I knew what I wanted. I didn't fool around."

136

"I still had the football, and I got into Bordentown Prep, a military school in New Jersey. They had a great football team. We won thirty-three in a row while I was there. Phil Sheridan went to Notre Dame, Joe Novogratz went to Pitt. They were both college captains and so was I. We had Paul Costa of the Bills on the team, and Tom Longo of the Giants. It was good football. I stayed two years there. I could have gone on to college after one year, but I didn't think I was ready to make it in college classes. After two years, I knew I was ready."

*Did you have trouble with studies at Syracuse?*

"A lot of people thought I would. Back in high school they had told me I only had an IQ of 100 and I could never cut it in college. That's why they gave me all the shops. But I went to Syracuse for an education. I played football all right, but I was there for the schooling. I went to summer school two years, so if things got rough in my junior and senior years I would have a little edge. And I took a double major, history and public relations. I was so far ahead that my senior year I had to look around for classes to take to stay eligible. And my grades were good enough that in my last semester I could have gotten three D's and an F and still graduated. See, by the time I got to college I was twenty years old. In my freshman dorm there were thirty-nine kids and only ten graduated. But when I got to Syracuse I knew what I wanted. I didn't fool around."

*You have your college degree now and you are in the midst of a successful career in pro ball. What would you like to do after football is over?*

"I've been thinking about going to law school. I suppose there's still people who think I couldn't make it, but I will. I wouldn't be the greatest lawyer, no Clarence Darrow or anything, but I could do a good job."

*You were talking about retiring earlier in the year.*

"I was upset at the time, but this turned out to be my best year. It would be hard to leave now."

*Don't you feel like you're stretching your luck? You'll be thirty this season.*

"No. I'm still strong."

*I suppose you've learned how to avoid the hard hits by now anyway.*

"No way. The way to avoid injuries is to go after people. I may not be that big, but I don't back off from anybody who puts on shoulder pads same as me. He may be bigger than me, but his heart works the same way. He can go down. When I'm playing football, I don't turn my back on anybody."

# Lynn Swann

## "Everybody on this squad is so good you have to play your best just to stay on the field."

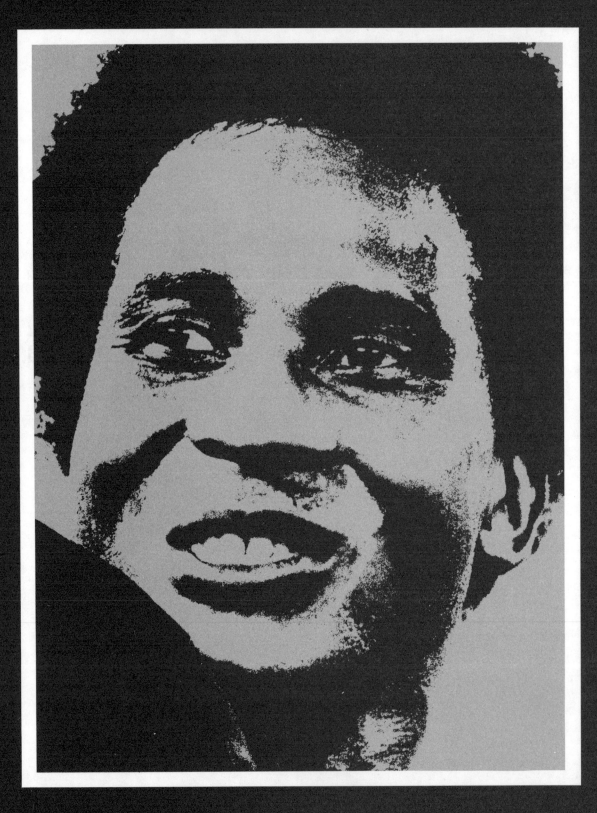

**"Faced with crisis, the man of character falls back upon himself."**

—*Charles de Gaulle*

Lynn Swann of the Pittsburgh Steelers is only one of twenty-two players when he lines up on the football field. But when the play starts, it looks like he's playing a game of his own. He is not very big, and he doesn't seem as quick as a wide receiver ought to be. Yet he does the impossible with great regularity.

His many brilliant Super Bowl catches are now a part of the collective consciousness of America. Swann connoisseurs, however, look back to a catch he made in college as his most remarkable. Going into the middle against Notre Dame, Swann leaped to take the ball chest high. While still in mid-air, he started to scissor his legs in one direction, then refined his calculations and scissored them another way. A tackler shot beneath him like a train screaming through a tunnel. Swann hit the ground running. It was a quintessential move for a man known for aerial feats.

One fascinating point about this artistry is that exceptional talent alone has not made for airborne acrobatics. As it happens, Swann has spent his life pursuing a wide variety of skills, from tap dancing to long jumping, a composite of capabilities that surfaces every time he leaps. Nothing is accidental, least of all genius.

And Swann, in this 1979 interview, brings out an even more compelling point. He expands the definition of human courage. In a book focused on pro football's gladiators, bravery might seem to mean only the willingness to expose one's body to physical assault. But Swann proves otherwise. In the turning point of his career, Swann had to show a more subtle—and sometimes elusive—type of fortitude. He had to stand up to his peers on a matter of principle. He had to hold out for his own opinions in the face of outspoken scorn. The incident reminds us that the courage of conviction is as admirable as its more obvious physical counterpart.

The interview starts at a much lighter place, however. At the behest of his questioner, Swann begins with a discussion of that astonishing Notre Dame catch.

"I remember that catch," he says. "I've often thought that was one of the great moves I ever came up with."

*How did you do it?*

"I don't know."

*What do you mean you don't know?*

"I was up in the air and here came this guy, and something just said to me, 'Open your legs.' So I did. It was instinct, a sixth sense."

*Do you always follow your instincts on the field?*

"I probably ought to. On that same play, after that guy flew under me, I had the feeling to hit the ground turning left. That was my instinct. But coming down I

# "It's helped a great deal. I think it has added style to my game."

had a chance to think about it and I changed my mind. I decided to go to the right. And I ran smack into the safety. If I'd turned the other way I had a touchdown."

*Still it was a pretty play. It almost looked like you were dancing.*

"Funny you should mention that. I've been dancing since I was in fourth grade."

*What type of dancing?*

"Tap dancing, mostly. Then some jazz, to help out with the tap, and then some ballet, to help out with the jazz."

*How did you get started?*

"I was a hyper kid. I think I was driving my mother a little crazy. And then, she always wanted a girl. She never had one, but I was the youngest boy, so I guess it was just me that got the dancing lessons and piano lessons. 'No football for *you*,' she said, and took me to tap lessons."

*You liked it?*

"A lot better than the piano. I liked working out all the steps. Maybe too much, in fact. Pretty soon mother was saying, 'You're going to ruin the *floor*.' 'But Mom, I got to practice.' 'Well, practice in the *bathroom* then.' So I did. And sitting at my desk at school, too."

*Your teachers must have loved that.*

"They didn't know. Tennis shoes don't make a lot of noise."

*Do you think the dance background has helped your football?*

"It's helped a great deal. I think it has added some style to my game. It's given my football some smoothness and coordina-

# "I was simply outraged that I had to suffer that type of blow."

tion. But then so did the gymnastics I did, and the trampoline work. And then my jumping was helped by all the basketball, hurdles and long jumping I used to do at school. It's all there in every catch."

*So your acrobatics are no accident.*

"No, there's a background to it. And a purpose, too."

*A purpose beyond just getting up in the air to meet the ball?*

"A lot of times there is. You can leap just to slow yourself down, for instance. Say I'm coming straight across the field on an 'in' route and the ball is thrown high and behind me. I may not have time to slow myself down and then jump. But if my timing is just right I can jump straight up hard, higher than I need to go. That slows me down, because my feet aren't down there driving any more. Then I get to the top of the jump and turn myself back to the ball and catch it on the way down."

*That's easy for you to say.*

"All you need is a little tap, and trampoline, and hurdles. Things like that."

*There's another thing a receiver needs: courage. You were once ready to give up the game because of being hit in the head.*

"But it wasn't clean hitting that bothered me. It was the cheap shots I objected to."

*There was a famous incident where you were pole-axed thirty yards away from the play. What were your thoughts when you considered your football future after that?*

"I was simply outraged that I had to

suffer that type of blow. I heard that some defensive backs called me a loud mouth and a cry baby because I didn't think mugging was football. And that got to me, too. I had to wonder if these were men playing pro football, or just people trying to prove their masculinity with this type of tactic."

*Why did you decide to go on playing?*

"After that season I went on a long trip around the world—Singapore, Japan, Kuwait. I wound up driving around in Europe by myself. And I was thinking if I should really subject myself to this type of abuse—this type of danger—just to play football. But finally it came to me. This was the first major challenge of my football career, really of my life as a whole. And I realized that if I stopped playing football without ever having met that challenge and overcome it, I wouldn't have lived a very happy life."

*You came back and made All-Pro and the League also changed the rules eventually. Do you think that has helped football?*

"I know it has. Due to the League's stand against violence most of the cheap shots have been done away with. If one goes undetected during a game, the player can be fined after the films are viewed. That's a strong deterrent. And what this has done is to force people to play a better brand of football. You can't defend against somebody just by knocking him dingy. Now the skills have to be there and the defense has to play a better thinking game.

# "There are some people who play very well just so they won't get embarrassed."

It's still a tough game, with all the drama and excitement and challenge you could want. But it's not a street fight."

*It must give you some satisfaction to have helped bring about this change.*

"It does. In some ways I felt like a pioneer. It wasn't popular and it wasn't easy. A lot of players believed in the unwritten law that if you don't get caught, it's legal. But instead of hiding behind the mask that football is a man's game—if you can't take it get out—I spoke out. And I'm glad I took a stand."

*Lynn, you've been on winning teams your whole career. What do you think it is that sets off a winner?*

"It comes down to one thing. A winner is someone who simply won't take anything less. He has to be the best."

*But why is that?*

"The reasons are different with each guy. It's like the Spanish Conquistadores who conquered Latin America for God, Gold and Glory. No one was sure what the highest priority was. It's the same with athletes. Some are there for the money, some for the fame, some for more significant reasons—to get some status so that people will listen when they try to help. And embarrassment is in there somewhere, too."

*Embarrassment?*

"It's a great motivator. There are some people who play very, very well just so they don't get embarrassed in front of their friends and a national audience."

*Anything else?*

"The guy behind you. There's nothing like competition to keep you going. That's one secret we have on the Steelers. Everybody on this squad is so good you have to keep playing your best just to stay on the field."

*Some people don't think competition is a good thing. They say it causes too much concern with winning and losing.*

"I think competition is healthy. It pushes you, makes you achieve your best. Maybe a guy thinks he's running all-out, but if he looks back and sees somebody gaining, he can find a little more speed. If there is nothing to force us beyond our own limits, we may never find out what we are capable of doing."

*So you'd recommend competition to everyone?*

"That and maybe tap dancing."

# Harry Carson

"I don't care if we win or lose,
I'm all out every down. Then if we lose, I'm square."

# Harry Carson

**"A man of courage is also full of faith."**
—*Cicero*

Harry Carson has come out of nowhere. Well, actually, he's come out of South Carolina State and the New York Giants got him on the fourth round in 1976. But that's close enough to nowhere, especially considering that Carson had never played middle linebacker before his pro arrival.

A nondescript and off-position background is highly unusual for a big-name pro middle linebacker. That's because the position is one of the most complex and demanding in any sport. In difficulty it approximates wrestling a bear in the middle of a freeway interchange while deciphering a computer print-out. As one of its practitioners says, "Eight or nine different guys may block on you in one game, sometimes two or three at a time. You never know who it's going to be or where they're going to come from." Such a position requires a tremendous athlete with a lot of experience, and for that reason you usually see the great ones coming for years before they make the pros. Dick Butkus, for instance, was Time magazine's "Animal of the Year" while still enrolled at Illinois.

But Harry Carson has gone from obscurity to All-Pro in just four seasons, and when you watch him it's easy to see why. Carson is all over the place, hitting people awfully hard. And when you talk to him, his driving exuberance comes over loud and clear. Like Don Maynard, Carson believes that attitude can get you anywhere, and his attitude may best be summed up as "belligerent exhilaration." He is a lively self-starter who makes Strong Thought seem far too tame a category. In this interview, Carson spends some time talking about the need to cultivate a positive intellect, to keep the mind quarantined from doubt and fear. But his first and basic point is more simply expressed.

"I just like to play football," he says. "In fact, I *love* to play football."

*All the time?*

"Every play, every game. I don't care if we're winning or losing. We can be behind fifty to nothing. I don't care. We're still playing football. I hate for the game to end."

*What accounts for this attitude?*

"That's just me, that's all. I just love being out there on the field. Sometimes I'll come back to the sidelines, and I'll reflect back on my past. I really don't know how I got here, I'll think, but I sure am enjoying it. There are so many guys who want to do this. I'm doing it. And I'm making it."

*Do you like everything about your life as a player?*

"No, I can't say that, truthfully. I don't like to practice, for instance. I'm not what they call a practice player. In fact, to be honest, I *hate* to practice. But come Sunday, that's my day. I live for Sundays."

*All day?*

"Well, no, I can't really say that either. I can't stand the morning routine, and all the waiting in the locker room, and the taping, and all that. But from the introductions to the gun, Sunday is a great day. If I had a wish, I'd wish every day was Sunday."

*The fun starts with the introductions?*

"Think about it. Your name booms out of the loudspeakers, you run into a stadium full of 75,000 people, your picture is flashing up on the scoreboard. Between one name and the next there's maybe ten or fifteen seconds—and it all belongs to you. You're on center stage. It's a great ego builder. It's a natural high."

*Does the cheering of the fans make you play any better once the game starts?*

"I get some strength from the fans. It's natural, knowing there are that many eyes on you, that many people cheering for you. I like to make them cheer. And I get some strength from my situation on the team. I'm the middle linebacker. The big plays in a game are expected from the quarterback and the middle linebacker. I know my teammates are depending on me. But most of my strength comes from somewhere else."

*Where is that?*

"From within. You just make it up in your own mind."

*Can't your coaches and your teammates give you strength?*

"Maybe. Sometimes. But you can't count on anybody outside yourself. All I can tell you about is me, not other people, and what I do is, I play a game within a game. I'm playing my own game out there—mine first, and then team ball."

*Coaches might not like to hear that.*

"Yeah, some people might object to that. But you have to see my situation. I'm playing on a team that hasn't been doing too well. We haven't been winning a whole lot since I got here. In a situation like that, players will talk pessimistically sometimes, and that can get you down, if you let it. Say a team hits us for a long pass. Some of our guys might get down, get discouraged. Now I try to keep them up. I'll be saying we can't tuck our tails and call it a day. Let's go. But my main thing is within myself. I'm going to put everything into every play, regardless. I don't care if we win or lose, I'm all out every down. Then if we lose, I'm square. I've done all I can do."

*What difference would it make, in a game that was long gone, if you eased up and coasted for the last few plays?*

"I used to have a sign hanging in my locker. It was the one that says, 'What you are is God's gift to you. What you make of yourself is your gift to God.'"

*You feel it's your duty to do your best?*

"This is where a religious attitude comes into focus. Everyone has a talent. Everybody in my family can do something well, for instance. They can sing or dance—they have some type of talent. Football is my talent, and I just believe that

whatever it is you can do, you should do the best you can. Put your all into it. If you don't utilize your talents, if you don't cultivate them, make them grow, then that's just a shame. It's a sin, really."

*Doesn't it ever get unpleasant, working hard to develop your talent?*

"No, see, it's just the most natural thing. Feeling your own strengths, that's where you get the feeling of self-satisfaction. Playing football to me, it's not work. It's not a way to earn a living. It's more like a hobby. Don't tell my employers, but sometimes I think I'd play for free. I really do."

*What's the most fun you get when the game is going?*

"A good hit. That's my game. I concentrate more on the running game because that's my strongest talent. And I just enjoy

# "Your head starts to expand. You get a lot of confidence. You can DO something."

making a bone-jarring tackle. I like to hear the fans go, 'Ooooohh.' "

*What's the pleasure of a good tackle?*

"Let's say a Walter Payton is coming to town. Here's a great running back, somebody I've only heard about or read about. Maybe I'm a little in awe of him. Then here he comes, and I have to stop him. If I can get one good hit on him, maybe I'll still respect him, but that awe starts to go. Here's this guy trying to run over me, and maybe I really get a pop, knock him a little silly. I see I can do it. That's Walter Payton on the ground. It's a great feeling, another ego booster. Your head starts to expand. You get a lot of confidence. You can *do* something."

*The confidence feels good?*

"And it makes you play better. It gets rid of doubt."

*What do you mean exactly by doubt?*

"Doubt is what makes you miss tackles."

*Why do you say that?*

"See, I've known players who put other players up on a pedestal. They think somebody else is way up there. I've even done it myself some. But there are two completely different attitudes you can take to a good opponent. One is, 'Uh oh, I'm playing this All-Pro on Sunday. I've seen him on TV. He must be good.' With that attitude you start to fear. You get afraid that you might *have* to tackle him. And that breaks your concentration. You don't get a good shot. The other approach is this: 'I've heard about this guy. We're going to have a good time. I'm going to get him out on the field and see what he's got.' Now that's a whole other thing. He has to handle *you*, then. That's the fun."

*And that's the attitude you have now?*

"It is. In the last couple of years, I've seen that other players now take *me* into account. They'll come up to me and say things after the game. Or one time I went to tackle a guy, and before I hit him, I saw he closed his eyes. He was bracing himself. This is a big name, he's a big, fast running back. And he closed his eyes. That surprised me. But it showed me something important."

*What's that?*

"There are no superhuman football players."

*You can't deny that some players are better than others.*

"But attitude can make the difference. In football—or in any sport, probably—it's not so much one team beating another team. The truth is that teams just beat themselves. They psyche themselves out. Think of that guy who closed his eyes. How can he get away from me if he can't see me? He gave up even before the tackle. And that's how it usually is with losers. They don't think they can win, so they don't. They get beat by doubt."

*So what is your advice to people?*

"Stop doubting."

*You think it's that easy?*

"It has to be. Otherwise it's somebody else running out there on Sunday."

# Larry Brown

**"There's only one thing I mind—the bench.
I hate the bench more than my worst enemy."**

# Larry Brown

**"Every man, however wise, needs the advice of some sagacious friend in the affairs of life."**

—*Plautus*

Larry Brown got to the top as a runner, but he had to take some back roads to get there. He had to go the blocking route. At a very young age he mastered the skill of taking out the linebacker, and coaches everywhere are enamored of this particular ability. Too much so, in Brown's case. They kept putting him in front of the ball, instead of giving it to him. His obscure hole-making status at the University of Kansas earned Brown only an eighth-round draft selection by the Washington Redskins, but when he arrived in Washington he finally found someone who would give him the ball. It was Vince Lombardi. The payoff was immediate. Under Lombardi, and then George Allen, Brown became pro football's premier runner of the early Seventies.

In a book seeking the winner's edge, Larry Brown makes a useful contribution. In the course of a highly individual interview, he reviews ideas that have recurred throughout. The main themes are there: the primacy of mind over the sheerly physical (Brown speaks of mental alertness, the winning attitude and the need for goals), the importance of all-out effort at every instant (he seemed to get more motivation from the spectre of the bench than MacBeth did from Banquo's ghost), and the crucial contribution of accurate assessment (like Russ Francis, Brown got his vital feedback from a coach, Vince Lombardi).

The Lombardi connection was fascinating. It was a meeting of a legend with a rookie, but more importantly, it was a match-up of men dedicated to excellence. The relationship wasn't simple, but it certainly was fruitful. To start with, Lombardi sized Brown up in football films and diagnosed, improbably, a debilitating hearing ailment Brown didn't even know he had. In addition, Lombardi analyzed Brown's running style and made suggestions that helped turn his halfback into a 1000-yard runner.

Brown himself did the rest. Charging recklessly through defenders like someone busting the wrong way up a highway, he broke that 1000-yard barrier in an era when few other backs did. It was an achievement he bore proudly.

"The thing that means the most to me is not that I've achieved something rare," he said at the time, "although this is important, too. Few people gain 1000 yards, few lead the NFL in running. But more important than that, I've achieved something that had previously been done by men I admire so much, Leroy Kelly, Gale Sayers and others. I expected to do it some day—I'm aware of my ability. I didn't think I'd do it so soon."

*What do you need to gain 1000 yards?*

# "I feel a man has to have goals to accomplish anything worthwhile."

"I feel a man has to have goals to accomplish anything worthwhile. My main goal is the same every year. I strive to make 100 yards in every game. I don't think I would make 100 yards very often if I didn't aim to do it. And I'm never satisfied unless it's well over 100. So I strive to get there as soon as possible each game."

*What do you do if you start slow?*

"It happens. Sometimes I have to settle for fourteen yards in the first half. Now, fourteen yards can be very depressing. But the important thing then is not to let it affect you. If you let it get you down, you won't do well in the second half, either. To win football games the main thing you've got to have is a winning attitude, and there's no time you need it more than when you've had an off day in the first half. And the same thing is true over the course of a whole season. The year can wear you down mentally, but there is no time you need to keep that winning attitude more than in the last few games."

*Why is that?*

"The hardest thing about 1000 yards a year is the last 300. The first 700 aren't bad. But after that, you find yourself taking three, four, five steps to cover as much ground as you used to get with half a step earlier in the season. Everybody is keying on you. It feels like when you move, the whole defense moves with you. In fact, when I look at the films, I can see that every move I made, whether I had the ball or not, brought one or two moves on the

other side immediately. Someone was keying on me all the time. It'll happen again this year, too. Those last 300 yards are going to come tough. I'll have to keep my goals high."

*Doesn't it get discouraging having to struggle so hard? How do you keep fighting against odds that heavy?*

"I don't mind the struggle. I don't mind the hitting. There's only one thing I mind,

# "The main thing I'm going to work on this year is to be more alert."

and that's the bench. That's probably why I became such a good blocker. I'll do anything to keep from sitting down. I hate the bench more than my worst enemy. I mean it. The thing that bothers me about an injury is not the pain, but the bench. I like to work hard at football and the reason I like to work hard is I despise the bench."

*In addition to hard work, however, a good back needs balance, speed, agility, strength, good hands. Which one do you work on most?*

"The most important thing is mental alertness. The main thing I'm going to work on this year is to be more alert. When the hole is closed in one place, I want to hunt for that second or third place quicker. Maybe I can even find a fourth place. The whole thing is being alert enough to find some daylight right now."

*What about physical abilities? Which is most important?*

"I work on being quick. Quickness is the salvation of a little back. I aim to get off with the ball every last time. When the other people begin to stir, I like to be in the hole and on my way out. There's no other way for a small runner to survive in the National Football League."

*If quickness is that important, isn't it surprising that you made the Redskin squad your first year? It wasn't until mid-season that Vince Lombardi discovered your ear trouble. Up until then it must have been hard for you to get into the holes on time.*

# "He yelled at me the way I suppose he yelled at Paul Hornung and Jim Taylor."

"I realize now that I was probably always late getting in there. I never knew there was anything wrong with my hearing and I thought I was getting off with the ball, but one day Coach Lombardi told me I was at least a half count late every time. He said he'd been studying films and that the ball was almost always in Sonny Jurgensen's hands before I started to move. I was looking at the ball before the play started. He told me to go get a hearing test."

*What did you think about that?*

"I was surprised. Nobody had ever mentioned anything about hearing to me. I told him I was probably a little slow getting off because I was trying to learn his system and trying to read the defenses at the same time. Coach Lombardi nodded."

*He just nodded?*

"He nodded, and smiled, and said go get a hearing test."

*What did the doctor tell you?*

"He said I was a medical marvel. He said I had a left ear that could make me famous. Watching television, for instance, my left ear is so remarkable that I hear almost as well as anybody with two good ears. All the tests proved that. But I'm nearly deaf in my right ear. So what happened was that voices coming from my right side were garbled in transition around to the left side. As a halfback, I usually stand on the left side of the quarterback, and I wasn't quite getting the signal."

*What kind of hearing aid did they make for you?*

"They put a receiver in the right side of my helmet and the speaker on the left, and connected the two with cords running across the top, over my head."

*The diagnosis of your hearing problem, when you had been playing football seven years and didn't even know you had one yourself, may have been one of Lombardi's greatest achievements.*

"He has been the most influential man in my life to date, and I'm sure I'll still be saying that fifty years from today. I knew it at the time, too. I knew he was the turning point for me."

*In those first days or weeks at training camp, when did Lombardi first become aware that there was a Larry Brown?*

"It happened in a nutcracker drill. I think that's where he discovered everybody. Or rather, that's where you had to prove it. That day, as usual, he had two big sandbags squeezing two big linemen together and as Sonny handed me the ball, I blasted by both linemen before they could raise up. Right there in front of God, Sonny, the two linemen and the two sandbags, coach Lombardi stopped practice and said, 'Nice going.' It was the most extravagant praise that had come out of him since he took over the Redskins. Right then—it was about the second week of training camp—I knew that if I worked hard, I was in."

*After that, did he try to reassure you and build your confidence?*

"No, he confused me as much as he ever did anybody else. I remember the day

"I began to hurt inside.
I was hurting with hate for this man."

# "It's exciting to be where you and everyone around you are trying their best."

he chewed me out so unfairly—I thought it was unfairly—that I began to hurt inside. I was hurting with hate for this man. Three, four days later he came up to me again—just as unexpectedly, and for no better reason that I could see—and put his hand on my back. 'Good play,' he said quietly. 'You're going to be a good back.' The thing is, he never treated me like a rookie. As soon as he began to pay attention to me at all, he treated me like a veteran. He expected the same quality of performance from me that he expected of a three-year veteran. At least, that's what I had to think, judging by the way he handled me and three-year veterans. I was just out of college and he treated me like a pro, yelling at me the way I suppose he yelled at Paul Hornung and Jim Taylor, the way I'd always heard he yelled. I appreciated being treated like a veteran at the same time I hated him for blistering me."

*What was the most important thing he taught you as a runner?*

"To find that hole. The whole Lombardi philosophy of carrying the ball is that if you can't find it, keep moving until you can. You see, there is a little more to this thing he called running to daylight than most people realize. He meant you do it in one continuous motion. He hated backs who took two steps in the same place—the dancers and prancers—the people who stop to look around. The trouble with being a fancy dan, he said, is that before you can find daylight, somebody finds you. "

*On balance, did you like Lombardi as a man?*

"That's hard to answer. There was never anything simple about your relationship with Lombardi. It was so hard to separate him personally from the man as a coach. I think I liked him. The kind of thing I admired was that he demanded the very best—and then some. That's a very appealing situation to me. It's exciting to be suddenly in a situation where you and everyone around you are trying their very best to do something well. To coach Lombardi, life was football and football was life. And I really think he considered loafing a worse sin than adultery. I never heard him put it quite this way, but this is the way he reasoned: show me a man who loafs and I'll show you a man who despises himself and all his teammates."

*And you agreed with that?*

"I did. I still do. I guess when it's all said and done, the reason I liked him is that hard work is my bag, too."

# Dewey Selmon

"It's inside yourself. You realize
there's something you just have to express."

# Dewey Selmon

**"The pious and just honoring of ourselves
may be thought the fountainhead from
whence every laudable and worthy enter-
prise issues forth."**

—*Milton*

**T**his is an interview with Dewey Selmon, of the Oklahoma Selmons. There
were three of them, brothers, playing
together on a national championship Oklahoma team several years ago. One of them
is still there, coaching the team, and two of
them, including Dewey, have gone on to
continue the brother act at the professional
level. Brother Leroy Selmon plays right defensive end for the Tampa Bay Buccaneers,
and he plays it so well that some are dis-
cussing him as the dominant defensive
athlete of the 1980s. Dewey Selmon lines
up about five yards away from his brother,
as an inside linebacker in the Tampa Bay
"3–4" defense. And Dewey is playing well
enough to have gained some All-Pro recognition of his own in his third season. He is
one of those athletes who seems always to
have location and timing in correct syn-
chrony, meaning he's usually where the
offense wishes he weren't, right then.

But the most interesting thing about
Dewey Selmon is what he does with his
non-football time. As this interview was
written in the spring of 1980, he was past
his Master's Degree and well on his way to
a Doctorate, and his field of study was, sur-

prisingly, philosophy. Few football players
study up on Aristotle and Kant, but then,
truth to tell, few of the rest of us do it
much either. Dewey Selmon is that rare
type who is seriously and systematically
thinking his way through life.

As such, he also makes a valuable contribution to a book on the winner's edge. A
score of All-Pros can tell us how to succeed once the rules of the game are estab-
lished. But Dewey Selmon asks questions
yet one step more fundamental. What game
should we play in the first place? Toward
what goal should our life be heading?

On the football field, these questions
may have simple answers. In the rest of
life, if we listen to Selmon, we could all
benefit from a little philosophy.

In an extensive interview, Selmon covers several other topics, as well. Like so
many other All-Pros, for instance, he
values highly the importance of teamwork,
of human cooperation, and he makes the
new point that the collective consciousness
of the team must avoid weakness just as
much as the individual consciousness of
any one player. And at the start of the discussion, it is no surprise to find a philo-
sopher-linebacker extolling the intellectual
side of football. When you ask him what
individual challenge of the game he enjoys
most, in fact, he replies,

"The mental aspect. The mental game
is the most fun and the most important."

*Why the most important?*

"If you are fortunate enough to get to

# "We spend 60% of our time preparing mentally, and only 40% physically."

the pros, you have the physical equipment. If you are going to get beat, you are going to get beat mentally."

*It seems obvious that coaches and quarterbacks have a great mental challenge. What's the mental load for a linebacker?*

"You have to get the edge on your opponents. You have to get smart enough that you know what they are going to do before they do it."

*How do you do that?*

"You study. In Tampa Bay, we think we have the smartest defense in football. We have eleven dedicated, well-prepared people. During the week, in fact, we spend 60% of our time preparing mentally, and only 40% physically. We take twenty-eight pages of tests every week. When we get out there on Sunday, we know what we're doing."

*What is it that you know?*

"The other team. We know all their plays, what they like to do where, which plays they run from which formations. I spend a lot of time Friday and Saturday just playing the game in my mind."

*Jack Youngblood has talked of the usefulness of visualization, of mental programming.*

"It's a powerful tool. I use it all the time. I spend so much time seeing their formations in my mind, and then watching the specific plays they run from those formations, that by game time when I see them line up, the right plays just come to

me automatically. '32 Blast, 38 Wide, 92 Pattern.' I hear the list in my mind as they get into their stance."

*And this is really a big advantage?*

"I'll say it is. You can play the game faster. You can stay one step ahead of the quarterback all the time."

*Do you have a good example of that?*

"Last year in the playoffs against Los Angeles. They were on our two-yard line and they came out in what we call the 'Western I' formation—with two tight ends and a close wingback. As soon as I saw that formation, I knew where they were going."

*Where?*

"Right at me. 32 Blast."

*What did you do?*

"I called out to my linemen—we have code words—and I had them all pinch into the two-hole right in front of me. The play got nothing. If you are prepared mentally like that, you can save yourself a lot of physical effort."

*Football, then, is primarily a mental challenge to you. Do you find this challenge at all parallel to your studies in philosophy?*

"Not really. I'm using the same mind, of course, but in philosophy I am using it to explore a completely different part of my self."

*There are two Dewey Selmons?*

"You could say that. In fact, I think that's a trend among professional football players. They aren't satisfied with one role anymore. It's like they are two people. One of them loves the game and wishes to excel at it, the other is almost a second identity —as a businessman, accountant, lawyer, whatever. My brother Leroy is a banker. I'm into philosophy. Players don't fit into one compartment anymore."

*Why is this trend developing?*

"A football player dies very fast."

*You don't mean literally.*

"No, but as a player. They have an average life span of four years, and then they're dead. And it's tough to live when you're dead. Right now, I'm Dewey Selmon, number 61. But one year out of uniform and where am I? Dead. So football players need a second identity, a second way to live. And you live by the works you do."

*Why did you choose philosophy?*

"Because of the mind expansion. In philosophy you study other ways of thinking, and you dig into your own self. It's a search for what our real meaning is. It's a way to expand your mind and develop the truth for yourself."

*Which philosophers do you enjoy the most?*

"The names that stick out are Plato and Augustine. They were thinkers who impress me, and their writings unite what we might call today both philosophy and theology. In later years philosophy narrowed down to cover only social ideas, ideas about society and politics. But earlier they were searching for complete answers, for divine truth. Not the truth of just one segment of life, but the truth of all of life."

*What's the attraction of Augustine, say?*

"He was fascinating. Very human but very spiritual. In his *Confessions* he tells his true story, of the way he tried faithfully to find the truth, of the way he'd find it, then lose it, then find it again, how he struggled against his own imperfections. He's honest and inspiring. He deals with the inner, spiritual make-up of a person."

*Do you think the study of philosophy has helped you in any specific way?*

"I know it has. I feel that through the study of philosophy I have found myself."

*What do you mean?*

"My whole direction has changed. When I first went to Oklahoma University

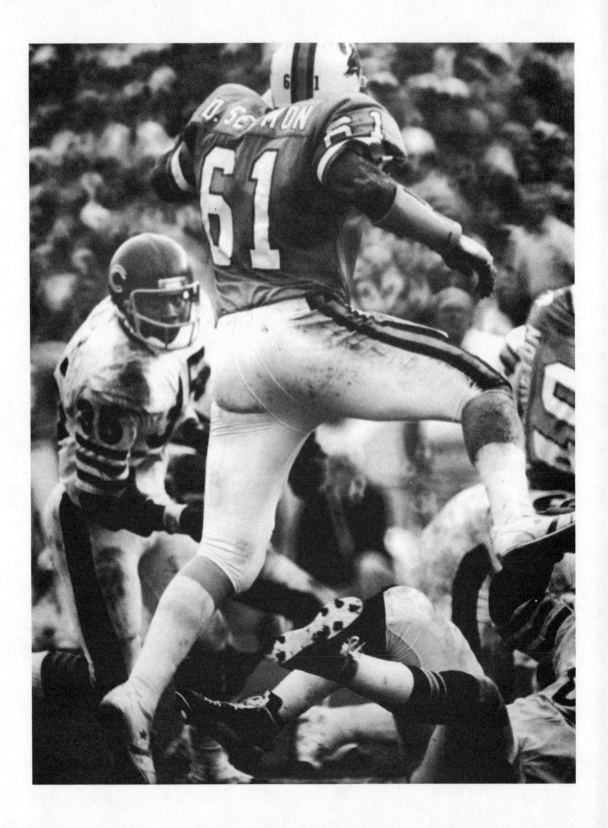

# "In philosophy you study other ways of thinking, and you dig into yourself."

163

I had it in my mind that I wanted to be a physical therapist. But as I started to study I found out that I was just playing a mind game on myself. I was trying to force myself that way. I'd tell myself that physical therapy was a good thing, that I could help people and earn a living. But what I found out was that it just wasn't *me*. It wasn't right for me. I had to completely reorganize myself."

*And philosophy helped?*

"It did. It helped me look into myself. And what I realized is that we need to know ourselves. We have to find what *we* are best suited for, and then go for that."

*There is that famous line from the Delphic Oracle, "Know Thyself."*

"This is the point. We have to know who we really are. If we pursue something that is not right for us, we won't be fulfilled. Take a simple example. I can play some basketball. I can dribble. I can shoot. But when I get to the college level, then I can't play that game. If I were to go after college basketball, I wouldn't have any fun. It would be a game, but I'd dread it."

*Having fun is important?*

"If you do what's right for you, then you have some success. And success is fun. We all need goals, but if you set a goal that you cannot achieve, then its unrewarding, and that's no good. I realized this one day when we were driving away from a game on the team bus. We passed a park and there were a bunch of guys out there having fun with a football. They were playing touch and going at it, and as far as I could tell they were having as much fun as I just had playing in front of 70,000 fans. You don't have to be a pro to do your best and enjoy it."

*How does one find out what's right for him?*

"This is the individual game we all get into with ourselves. I believe that every person has some reason for being here. Each individual has certain potentials, some things he is definitely good at. The game is to figure them out, to figure out what is our *best* goal. Then we go for that, we master that."

*How do you know when you've found the right goal?*

"If you try to go too fast, it can be confusing. There are all these things that can sidetrack a person—what other people think, the need for money. But if you approach it from a slow point of view—taking time to develop yourself physically and mentally—you'll find your direction."

*There are some false starts?*

"Usually, I'm sure. I want to master a lot of things, for instance—physically and mentally—but they don't all stick. I remember one summer I wanted to master a new skill. So I took a job laying carpet. I was at it two weeks and I realized, 'Hey, I've got this cold.' And I quit. That was all I wanted—to master it. But you have to keep doing things like that. You have to expand yourself physically, expand yourself mentally, do different things. Then it'll come."

# "Mental toughness. The strength to know yourself, to know your own truth."

*How do you know when you've found the right thing?*

"You know. It's inside yourself. You realize there's something inside you that you just have to express. There's something there that just tells you you have to do it. Other people may not even feel what you do is very good. But if you enjoy it, if you get that satisfaction, then you do it."

*What direction do you think you'll take?*

"I feel fortunate that I have a number of things open to me. But one of them stands out."

*What's that?*

"Writing."

*Philosophical writing?*

"Yes. There are things I've had a chance to find out, and I feel I should pass them on. This is the thing that's inside me, that needs to be expressed. I'll do a book. Maybe it will collect dust on the shelf, maybe it will be studied. But I have to do it."

*What if you ignore this impulse?*

"I won't. I'd be less of a man if I didn't do it. I feel I must write. And I shall. And I shall be known by my writing."

*Talking to you makes philosophy seem as exciting and challenging as football. Still, it's an unusual combination in anyone. Which activity is more satisfying to you?*

"Football is intense. But football offers enjoyment that only lasts a fraction of a lifetime. And there's a part of it you dread."

*Which part?*

"The physical toll. It's rough. There's no football player who would tell you they want to take that physical abuse for a whole lifetime."

*But the football does provide a great challenge.*

"It does. But think of Plato and Augustine. They took their whole lives as a challenge—to search for truth, to study and teach philosophy. It's always challenging. You can continually do better."

*Many people think that football teaches important lessons about life. Do you think that the game is important philosophically?*

"You can learn from the game. In fact, I used to think that when I had a son, for sure I'd want him to play football, to learn those lessons. But as I've grown, I've seen that many of the lessons of football can be learned other ways. A good football player learns that you never give up, for example. But think of Mozart, one of the best composers ever. Not too many people thought much of him in his time. But he knew his talent in himself. He persisted. He didn't give up. You can learn that lesson many places in life. Or if my son wants a challenge, for instance, he can get a watch, set it, and run a mile every day. He can compete with himself. Because it's all in yourself. Even the toughness you learn in football, you can develop that in a more important way off the field."

*What sort of toughness?*

"Mental toughness. The strength to know yourself, to know your own truth, and to put that forth even when others tell you you're wrong. It's that consistency in yourself."

*So you wouldn't encourage your son to play football?*

"What I'm saying is that now I'll leave it completely up to him. As my philosophy has developed, as I've taken note of things around me, I've found that football takes second place to mind. So if my son decides not to play, I'll have no qualms."

*And you don't think he'll miss anything important?*

"He'll be his own man, that's my point. I won't be able to speak for him. My truth is true only for myself. But if I do speak about my own experience, I have to say one thing. There is one aspect to football that I have found not only enjoyable but truly valuable."

# "Really it's like there is just one mind for eleven people."

*What is that?*

"It's the team experience, the unity experience. It's when you finally reach the point where you are just one of eleven guys on the field, that you are working together as one unit—and that you're winning."

*Why do players keep bringing that up?*

"Nothing else compares to it. Last year we had eleven guys on defense, eleven strong individuals who played as a team. There was no separateness on the field. The play would start and it was like one body moving out there. It's a feeling that, once you've had it, you value highly."

*Working together feels that good?*

"I've realized both extremes. I've been at Tampa Bay when there was no cohesion at all. It was the pits. I played for myself. Everybody else played for himself. And we got beat."

*That seems like a clear lesson.*

"It is. If you can't give up yourself to the team, you can't play this game. You cannot say, 'Hey, I'm going to do things my way and get myself some glory.' You mess up the whole defensive scheme. On a team like that, guys are always making mistakes and guys are always hollering at each other. And nobody is winning. The only way for a football team to win is for every guy to say that his own self is secondary, that the team is first. Then you get cohesion. Then you get unity. On a team like that, when somebody makes a mistake, nobody puts him down for it."

*What does happen?*

"Ten other guys cover for him."

*There's a feeling of brotherhood?*

"Really it's like there is just one mind for eleven people. One mind thinking about the next play. And when you get that, you begin to develop the idea that you'll never think about losing. You just don't think about it. Not one player."

*Couldn't ten other players make up for one negative attitude?*

"Even one is dangerous. If you think about losing, it spreads. Every football team has to have a goal, and that goal is winning. If anybody thinks negative, if somebody finds himself feeling, 'Man, let's get this over with,' then the other team has the edge on you."

*A psychological edge?*

"The winner's edge. It's the mind that counts."

# Frank Ryan

"The most important thing for a quarterback is to remain stable under all that pressure."

# Frank Ryan

**"As a man's mind is, that is how he is."**
— *Cicero*

I first met Frank Ryan when he was a twenty-year-old rookie with the Los Angeles Rams and I was a teenaged jack-of-all-trades at the team's summer training camp in Redlands, California. He was, immediately, a man who stood out from the crowd. In the first place, he had a rather extensive and regular correspondence, almost all of it chess games he was playing by mail. In the second place, he went through the basic trials and tribulations of a rookie with the bemused, analytic attitude of a helmeted Hamlet. Talking football with Frank was like taking a course in exploratory philosophy. I liked it then and I still like it today, and it was a great pleasure for me to write this article on him which first appeared, in a somewhat different form, in PRO! magazine several years ago.

This is not just an interview, but a personality piece with some interview interspersed. If anyone deserves the extra space, and this culminating place in the book, it is Frank. In an upwardly mobile on-field career that crested at championship status, Ryan learned the best lessons of football. He has put them to use in a rich and varied post-football career.

Ryan ties this book off in another way as well. There is no one I know who has more powerful thought at the basis of his life, more energy and focus in his daily activity, or a greater capacity for searching assessment of every aspect of his existence. He may never have heard of Christopher Attwood, but he certainly lives the Triangle of Success more fully than most. (Editor's note: As this book is published, Frank has moved from the thoroughly conquered job in Washington described here to the Athletic Director's office at Yale University.)

Frank Ryan arrives at his office in the Longworth House Office Building, early as usual, and sits down to a list of tasks waiting on his desk. He and the 200-man staff he has built during the past several years are in charge of the installation of a million-dollar voting system in the United States House of Representatives. The project is something of an electronic revolution in the history of democracy, and the work has been tense and time consuming.

But before he can begin work on his list of problems this morning, he opens two letters that start his day with a smile. One of the letters is from an eastern college, offering him a job as head of the mathematics department. The other is from an eight-year-old boy, asking for diagrams for two sure-fire touchdown plays.

In the last decade, only seven men have been world champion quarterbacks. The select group has included some of the most skillful people who have ever played

# He resembles a piano virtuoso
# who doubles as a weight lifter.

the position, athletes who have thrown accurately, thought clearly and led their teams with contagious confidence.

But even allowing for the wide range of abilities all these champions have shown on the football field, one of the seven stands out as a truly multi-talented human being. Frank Ryan earned a Ph.D. in mathematics while also fashioning his professional football career. He has written a complex computer program for football strategy which is now being used by two teams in the NFL. He has spent six years as a university professor, and he is now filling an important post in Washington, D.C. as director of the rapidly growing computer systems for the House of Representatives.

If Frank Ryan were an athlete who was also a dancer, or a mathematician who was also a chess whiz, it would be more understandable. But Ryan's skills don't all fit into one compartment. He resembles a piano virtuoso who doubles as a weight-lifter. He has exceptional talents —physically, mentally and in human relations—and he also has the kind of energy and drive that push him working far into the night. Most of us usually look for ways to back off and rest, but Ryan is always seeking new problems to solve, new ways to challenge his skills. He abhors idle time the way nature abhors a vacuum and his life seems to be a race between the great gifts he was given and his determination not to waste any of them. Dr. Frank Ryan is not an ordinary championship quarterback.

In 1964 and 1965, Ryan led the Cleveland Browns to two consecutive divisional titles and their only world championship between 1957 and the present day. It was a sweet reward after years of largely empty effort. Success had not come easy to him. At Rice University he played second-string through most of his four varsity years and he spent four frustrating seasons with the Los Angeles Rams, seasons when he played enough to make mistakes but not enough to profit from them.

But then Ryan went to Cleveland, and his dedication to a difficult sport paid off. The strong-armed quarterback and his wide receivers, Gary Collins and Paul Warfield, practiced themselves into the most devastating long passing attack since the mid-century Rams of Waterfield, Van Brocklin, Fears and Hirsch. With fullback Jim Brown averaging something like a mile a year overland, the Cleveland offense was a weekly explosion and the team soared to two consecutive Eastern division titles.

In the first of those title seasons, 1964, the Browns went up against Johnny Unitas and the Baltimore Colts for the NFL championship. In a memorable upset, the Cleveland defense sealed Unitas out of the end zone while Ryan delivered three scoring passes to Collins. At the end it was 27–0. With luck, hard work and some help from his friends, Frank Ryan had reached the top of one of his professions.

# "I would prepare my psychology in advance. I worked on my mind all week."

It's not surprising that when Frank Ryan looks back at football as he played it, he puts the major emphasis on the role of the mind. Before he thought up his job as head of House Information Systems, he almost literally thought himself up as a championship quarterback. And in his opinion it was the coach he met in Cleveland, Blanton Collier, who got him started on this road.

"Collier did something very fundamental," he says. "He taught me the proper focus, the ability to concentrate under pressure."

*What were his methods?*

"He had a series of gimmicks, tricks to narrow the range of things you allowed yourself to concentrate on. If I was throwing the ball to a receiver, for instance, he didn't want me thinking about that receiver in just a general, unfocused way. If I did that, the ball might go out in just the general direction. His idea was to focus down, to throw the ball at a specific target like a shoulder pad or face mask. As the target got smaller, the concentration became more intense."

*Do you think it worked?*

"I'm sure it did. It almost got to where you were in a trance. All you had your mind on was this thought about throwing the ball to a certain spot. Then, without even being conscious of doing it, the ball would just go out there. It was a dramatic effect, and it led me to re-evaluate my whole approach to the game."

*What do you mean?*

"The most important thing for a quarterback is to remain stable psychologically under all that pressure. It's not easy. Big people are pounding you around. You make mistakes. The ball bounces funny. You have to be able to maintain your evenness in all this confusion."

*How did you do it?*

"My trick was to prepare my psychology in advance. I worked on my mind all week every week."

*Other players have spoken of visualizing their play in advance.*

"I'd do that. I'd think about defenses,

# "It was an optimal procedure, I thought, for avoiding the psychology of error."

172

visualize my receivers, imagine the ball going out. I would create the whole situation in advance. But there was something I did that I thought was even more important."

*What was that?*

"I'd imagine ahead of time all the states of mind I might get into, and what to do for each different state."

*Can you explain what you mean exactly?*

"I'd get ready for the time I might throw an interception, for instance. I'd rehearse what I should do with my mind. I'd think about how I should feel coming off the field, what I should think about sitting on the bench. The idea was to establish a peaceful countenance and to be ready to fight myself out of trouble mentally."

*Mistakes can be depressing. How could you fight those negative thoughts?*

"I'd prepare whole streams of thoughts to have when I got into difficulty. It was keyed to an analysis of the basics. First, I would find out what error I had made—throwing poorly, misreading the defense, whatever. Then, because of my preparation, this would bring up the next stream of concentration: all the thoughts about the fundamentals of throwing, for example—footwork, balance, arm action. It was an optimal procedure, I thought, for concentrating on useful thoughts and avoiding the psychology of error."

*Would you keep on thinking this way when you got back on the field?*

"I wouldn't have time then. But all the preparations would be there, just below the surface of consciousness, where it could affect activity."

*Athletes spend a lot of time training their bodies. But you were training your mind.*

"That was it. The goal was to have a mind completely trustworthy. It was an interesting challenge."

The Director of House Information Systems sits in his aged wood and leather office. The view from his window is typically Washingtonian: cold, austere, and brooding with power. Dr. Frank leans back behind his old round-corner desk with his salt-and-pepper hair thatching long over his ears and a large cigar angling out of his mouth. He has something of the look of an old-line politician, except when a mischievous glint hits his eyes and a gleeful cackling laugh cracks out of him.

His new responsibilities have revealed him to be a sober and tactful man, comfortably at home in his dealings with both politicians and technicians, but his delightful little boy's sense of humor is still there. In an earlier incarnation, Frank Ryan, No. 13, was known as one of the classy locker room pranksters in pro football annals and it is still his childlike humor and sense of wonder that add the perfect counterpoint to his sense of drive and total commitment. Even the smallest novelty can flash him back to that boyhood state of excited dis-

# It seems almost necessary to blow
# up your own rocket in your own garage.

covery when everything is new and it seems almost necessary to blow up your own rocketship in your own garage just to be personally involved in the adventure. Yes, Frank Ryan did do that, too.

A discussion begins on the details of the revolutionary computer-aided electronic voting system that is being installed in the House chamber with the help of the Control Data Corporation. "The traditional roll call system can take an ungodly amount of time," Ryan says. "There are 435 members in the House and by the time the clerk calls all the names and then goes back through the list again to get those who were missing or passed their vote the first time, it can take forty-five minutes to get the vote counted. Three or four roll calls can knock a hell of a hole in the working day."

Ryan starts a sentence on the wonders of the new system he is installing, but then suddenly stops, staring down at the two rubber bands he has been fiddling with. "God, that's clever," he says. He jumps out of his chair and comes around to share his discovery. He has the two rubber bands linked together so that when he pulls the two inner loops towards the outside, the link pattern disappears and then reappears as a mirror image of itself. "Isn't that amazing," he says, sliding the bands back and forth. "I never knew you could do that."

Just as quickly, he is back behind his desk carrying on his earlier line of thought. "With the computer system," he says, "it

should only take fifteen minutes to get a vote. It could take less, but some Representatives have offices nearly fifteen minutes walk-time from the chamber."

Every Representative will be issued a hole-encoded identification card. When a vote is called, he will insert his card into one of the many voting stations located in the House chamber and then cast his vote. The result will be shown immediately on the "scoreboards" overhead. An additional feature of the system will be in the three small video screens installed at the desks of the Speaker of the House and the legislative leaders for the political parties. The Democratic leader could, for instance, request on his video screen a complete list of all Democrats who had not yet voted on an issue in progress, or a list of Republicans who have voted "yea."

With the backing of the Committee on House Information, Ryan has been working on the project for over a year and the installation is virtually complete now although he doesn't expect the House to use it officially until the new session in January. He is impatient to witness the product of this effort. If the electronic voting system functions smoothly, computer assistance to the legislative process will receive a big boost. There is currently a wide gap between the analytical capabilities of the legislative and executive branches of the federal government. While the executive branch of the government employs over 4,000 computers in fulfilling its re-

sponsibilities, the House and Senate each have one medium-sized computer.

"In a sense," says Ryan, "the electronic voting system has to work better than any computer system ever built. We can't afford a single error in voter identification or information retrieval. We have built into the design an entire back-up monitor system which kicks in automatically if the master computer fails. But even that isn't foolproof; for example, what happens if the monitor system malfunctions and asserts itself when it shouldn't? This is the type of problem my staff has to solve, and the committee and I are fortunate to be supported by a really quality staff."

At this somber stage in the conversation, one of Ryan's secretaries arrives with something that lightens his mood immediately. It is a cup of coffee. He raises it up near his cheek as he adds a teaspoon of sugar. "I love the way sugar sounds when it goes into coffee," says Dr. Frank Ryan.

"Dr. Ryan is usually here before we are," says one of his secretaries, Betty Sharp. "He is very considerate, but most of the time he seems to be lost in deep thought. He often loses track of time and usually when he comes in in the morning he doesn't think to turn on the lights. We come in and turn them on and there he is just working."

For the first time in his life, Ryan has one single challenge which consumes all his working time. "This is not an easy job

at all," he says. "It used to be that I was doing two things at once—playing football and going to school, or teaching math and working on the football program. But I can't do that now. We could all work in here eighty hours a week and not make a dent in the job."

Not only has Ryan had to supervise the design and installation of the precedent-setting electronic voting system, but he has also had to build a specialized staff from scratch and spend a great deal of time studying further ways to use computers to help the House. For example, computer technology could aid the legislators in drafting and researching bills and law. The vast information retrieval capability of computers can provide Congress with increased ability to meet its responsibilities.

"Nobody has yet adapted computers in a sophisticated way to the legislative process," Ryan says. "It takes a lot of thought and a lot of good people. I've burned a lot of brain cells over this thing."

Fortunately for both Ryan and the House, he is a man who loves to spend his time thinking. He has spent years honing his mind on the magic rigors of mathematics, constructing elaborate air castles based on the most demanding of laws but built only in the abstractions of the mind. "Solving a math problem," he says, "is sometimes like writing a good poem in a foreign language that few people understand."

As complex as thinking on his new job appears to be, it can hardly be more de-

# "It's like crawling across the packed sands of the Sahara for two days."

176

manding than those deep journeys down the trackless tunnels of complex variables, real analysis and topology. "The solution to a problem in mathematics can take years," Ryan says. "You have to take all the elements, shape them neatly and then exhaust all the possibilities for solution. It can be unbelievably frustrating to try everything you have ever read, everything you can come up with within yourself, and still not get a solution. You just have to stay with it and finally you reach the point that makes it all worth it—that great moment of 'Aha!'—the instant when you've found the trick that will get you out of your trap. It's like crawling across the packed sands of the Sahara desert for two whole days and nights and then finally reaching water."

When he was working on his Ph.D. dissertation, his "Aha!" came at 3 a.m., when he was flat on his back in bed. He pounded on the bed, jarring his wife, Joan, out of a deep sleep, hollered out, "I've got it!," and stormed out to the mathematics building to write up his solution.

"Solving a math problem has always been a great feeling for me," he says, "probably because I've solved so few." He laughs his little boy laugh, and then adds a thought that is typical of him, a thought that explains much of his life.

"When you finally reach the solution," he says, "it is very self-supporting. It confirms in your mind that you *can* do it, that if you try hard and keep chipping away,

you'll get there. A proper solution validates all your effort."

You could never call Frank Ryan a quitter. And when he thinks about it, he feels that football has had a lot to do with this.

"Joan and I were talking about this just the other night. I never had anything given to me in football. Maybe no player ever does. First you have to make the team. Then you have to make the starting lineup. Then there's the real challenge: maintaining quality performance over time. One thing I'm sure I got from this is the attitude that you earn what you get and you get what you earn."

*Do you think football teaches you such a lesson where other aspects of life might not?*

"Yes. I think there are a lot of places where the connections get vague. In big, bureaucratic companies, for instance, people can get just submerged. A lot of people come in every day and function fairly well, but the only progress they make is just the nominal, automatic advancements built into the structure. They just move along on the current of the system."

*Football is different?*

"In football you have specific, clear goals, obvious things you can achieve with work. If you are not yet the starting quarterback, you know what you want out of life. It gives you a focus. It gives you that incentive to work hard, the carrot pulling the mule."

# "I'm looking for people who make things happen, who create excitement."

*And this attitude has carried over into your current life?*

"It's definitely a theme I see nowadays in my work. And it's not just the approach I take to my own tasks. I find myself very impatient with people who just settle into a job and punch the time clock. I'm looking for people who make things happen, people who are interested in creating excitement. This is another way that I think football, especially pro football, influenced me."

*What do you mean?*

"In pro football, and especially on a championship team, you are surrounded by a group of people each of whom is highly qualified. These are really good athletes. You know you can depend on them, that you can exploit their skills for the good of the whole team. This structures a certain level of expectation, and what I have found is that when I got involved in an institutional bureaucracy the cast of characters is, shall we say, not always superlative."

*What have you done about that?*

"This place is something of a merry-go-round. There are a lot of people we bring in here who put in only a couple of months before they have a chance to seek further employment. I find I use exactly the same approach I would in football: do the people have talent, and do they show it in their daily performance? My experience has left me with a keen sense of both."

*So there is no doubt that your football years have had a positive carry-over effect on your life?*

# "Winning that championship leaves you with a deep sense of confidence."

"None at all."

*How important do you think it was to win the championship?*

"It made a difference, I'm sure. If we hadn't won it, it probably would have taken the edge off that whole career. Winning that championship leaves you with a deep sense of confidence; you have been able to come through a particular set of difficult circumstances. It leaves you with the sense of being completely successful. But the championship only intensifies what sports do for you anyway."

*What are you speaking of specifically?*

"That emotional payoff and satisfaction that comes from achieving some clear accomplishment."

*But people can do this in their daily lives.*

"It's not easy anymore. Modern society is too complex. There are too many variables to deal with. Nothing is simple and clear-cut because we take in so much information on all sides of an issue through newspapers, the television, the telephone, traveling. Should we get a big car for our family, or a small car to save gas, or give up on cars and use roller skates? On most questions today it's hard to say that we can get anywhere close to being right."

*What's different about sports?*

"The charm of sports is that you have a small set of rules, a limited set of boundaries. In basketball, say, the main object is obvious: make the ball go through the hoop. This is achievable. You can do it.

And that sense of achievement leads to great happiness. This is one reason so many people go on playing sports after college. Maybe their daily lives are confusing, unrewarding, with relentless pressure. But they get into a pick-up half-court game and they can drive for a lay-up, steal a pass, make some good shots. They can make things happen. It's an exhilarating experience."

Joan Ryan is an attractive blond, with clean good looks and a southern courtesy that seem to fit naturally into the Ryans' grand old two-story house outside of Washington. Every time the family moves, Joan gets them into an older house because she likes the feeling of living with history.

She is the mother of four sons—Michael, Pancho, Stuart and Heberden—who are notable to a visitor chiefly for their intelligence and considerate manners. She is also Frank Ryan's closest and most appreciative observer.

"Frank can be a very determined man," Joan says. "Maybe it's because he was always the underdog. He was second-string at Rice most of the time and then we just went through hell in Los Angeles. I'm not sure why—but I do know that when Frank gets blood in his eye, he's going to get his job done."

After the conclusion of the 1970 season Ryan faced a problem that all athletes face when their playing days end—how to find a career. Of course the problem wasn't

"It confirms that you can do it.
A proper solution validates your effort."

# An ex-quarterback had helped
# democracy into the Twentieth century.

180

quite the same for Frank as for most others. In the first place he already had a second career, as a mathematics professor. He loved that job, but had begun to feel that it was too private a pleasure, that it didn't help enough other people. In the second place, the demands he would make of his new job were not those the normal person might make.

Joan encouraged him that winter to sit down and discuss a list of criteria that his new job would have to meet. They sat up together late one night. "The primary concern," as Joan remembers, "was that the new job have a back-to-the-wall aspect, a brinksmanship aspect. Then it had to give Frank some large area of responsibility, it had to be aimed at the concerns of many other people than just us, it would hopefully be out of the publicity glare, it had to pay some money and it had to lead to some natural career goals."

This was an ambitious list and it was not at all obvious where such a job would come from. But Joan feels that "vocalizing" the goals made things clear in Frank's mind and in a matter of months he had been offered the House job. With the new electronic voting system hanging fire immediately, the job filled every requirement. Frank took it and began to build.

At first, the House wanted to hire Ryan alone. The tradition-bound lawmakers weren't really sure just how much of this new-fangled computer stuff they really wanted to deal with. Ryan not only saw the need, however; he also had the drive and the diplomacy to convince the Representatives. Within a matter of days he had a staff of four. Within two years, he had his team of 200. An ex-quarterback had helped democracy into the twentieth century.

In Joan's eyes, this success is just the latest in a remarkable series of accomplishments by her husband and the admiration she feels for him is unfeigned. She has even considered writing a book about his life.

"I've got a title for it," she says, and she is unabashed by either the pun involved or the hero worship. "I'll call it 'The Upward Spiral.' "

Frank Ryan is throwing a football. He has his back to the large house and he is throwing down a gentle grass slope to his four sons. Every pass is a crisp spiral slicing to ready hands. All of his receivers are energetically accomplished. This is a family that has played a lot of catch.

"I particularly like to throw the football," Ryan says. "I think I'd rather throw the ball than do anything else. It's an aesthetic thing—having a clean motion and throwing a spiral that has some snap to it."

When Ryan first came to the pros, he had a weird wrist whip to his throw like no other quarterback. "I think I got that whip because of a challenge I made to myself when I was about twelve," he says. "I watched other boys throwing long passes and they had to take skip steps and go

# On his lawn he can still lay out
# an attractive pass for his boys to chase.

through a lot of gyrations to get the ball out there. I was sort of disdainful of them because they didn't throw the ball in a pretty way. So I challenged myself that I would never have to take more than one step to throw the ball, no matter how long the pass. I developed that unusual whip in my throwing motion to get the distance. I never was a great short passer, but I believe I was deadly on those deep post and corner passes."

His arm and shoulder hurt him now, and every throw brings a little grimace. On his lawn in the late afternoon sun, he can still lay out an attractive pass for his boys to chase. But those monstrous 70-yard bombs to Collins and Warfield are just memories and his days with football's professionals are done.

Dr. Frank Ryan has moved on to other challenges.

# Reprise: The Triangle Of Success

After twenty strong men give twenty different slants on success, a review is in order. What were the best points made? What are the most useful ideas to recall in the next mini-crisis of daily life?

Everybody would make his own list of quotes, naturally, and any selection can only be incomplete. Since I enjoy thinking with these athletes, however, I'm going to lay out one set of choices. I hope they prove of worth to the reader.

For the sake of consistency, I have arranged the quotes under the three headings of the Triangle of Success. I have not done this lightly. Though there are many different ways to account for success, I have become increasingly impressed with the usefulness of Christopher Attwood's theory as I have continued to work on this book. The Triangle is both sensible and practical. And in this book it's easy to find the quotes to flesh it out.

The aim here is condensation and impact. If people have enjoyed reading the interviews in this book, then I'll be happy. And if they gain some inspiration from the sum of it, if they feel—even a little—like jumping up and down and getting more out of life, then I'll be even more fulfilled.

## Strong Thought

"There are usually one or two guys around who can carry a team, who set the tone for a whole football game. . . . I believe I can do it, too."

"A man of character knows what his limitations are—but he doesn't accept them."

"Every Sunday we go out there and Reggie says, 'We can *beat* these guys.' And he means it. And he gets other people to believe it."

—O. J. Simpson

"Every play you are the one that has to wear the hat. You have to make it happen."

"I was always confident. I knew I just had to take hold of that situation. The test was how well I would meet that particular challenge. And I wanted that test."

—Joe Greene

"I'm a believer now. If I'm doing what I have to do, . . . I don't feel I can be beaten."

"If I can beat a guy in his mind, everything else falls into place."

—Dan Dierdorf

"You can have all the intelligence in the world, be Phi Beta Kappa, collect college degrees, and it means nothing if you can't control it."

"I visualize things in my mind before I have to do them. It's like having a mental workshop. . . . It keeps you a step ahead."

"I honestly believe that if a man has talent, and he learns how to control his intelligence and direct that talent, the sky is the limit."

—*Jack Youngblood*

"If you take it easy for ten minutes, it takes a long time to get it back, sometimes a week or two. Like everything else, concentration is a habit."

"At the beginning of each new play, I think of it as the most important play of the year. I go into it as if the game depends on it."

—*Merlin Olsen*

"What I do is prepare myself until I know I can do what I have to do. Then I have faith."

"The goal is to get my mind geared up to where everything just goes click-click-click. Wait a minute, something's moving differently out there. Boom! Jump on it."

—*Joe Namath*

"The coaches didn't call it a drop, but I did. And that's the way I'll keep it."

"I believe football is 10% physical and 90% mental attitude. . It's amazing what guys can do, or *could* do, if they just have the right attitude."

—*Don Maynard*

"In order to win, you must *expect* to win. . . . You might even call it the arrogance factor."

"The key is to concentrate your way through the bad times. . . . And I really believe that you can have some of your best games that way. You play better because you have to concentrate harder."

—*Dan Fouts*

"Even before I was hurt, I had prepared myself. I decided that if I ever got a knee, I would come all the way back the very next year."

—*Gayle Sayers*

"I was smart enough to know that I wasn't failing to get the job because I was black. I was failing because I couldn't read the tests. . . . But I also knew I was going to come back and make it."

"He may be bigger than me, but his heart works the same way. He can go down. When I'm playing football, I don't turn my back on anybody."

—*Floyd Little*

"Doubt is what makes you miss tackles."

"My strength comes from within. You just make it up in your own mind."

"Teams just beat themselves. They psyche themselves out. . . . They don't think they can win, so they don't. They get beat by doubt."

—*Harry Carson*

"I feel a man has to have goals to achieve anything worthwhile. I don't think I would make 100 yards in a game very often if I didn't aim to do it."

"To win football games the main thing you've got to have is a winning attitude, and there's no time you need it more than when you've had an off day in the first half."

—*Larry Brown*

"This was the first major challenge of my football career, really of my life as a whole. And I realized that if I stopped playing football without ever having met that challenge and overcome it, I wouldn't have lived a very happy life."

—*Lynn Swann*

"During the week we spend 60% of our time preparing mentally, and only 40% physically. We take twenty-eight pages of tests every week. When we get out there on Sunday, we know what we're doing."

"Mental toughness. The strength to know yourself, to know your own truth, and to put that forth even when others tell you you're wrong. It's that consistency in yourself."

—*Dewey Selmon*

"My trick was to prepare my psychology in advance. I worked on my mind all week every week. . . . The goal was to have a mind completely trustworthy. It was an interesting challenge."

—*Frank Ryan*

# Dynamic Action

"My definition of a good runner is that he's *insane*—he does wild things, stuff you never see, and he does it spontaneously. Even he doesn't know what he's going to do next."

—*O. J. Simpson*

"You are full of a feeling of power, of confidence, of *superior* confidence. You reach a peak in every part of your being. You reach an emotional high, a physical high, a mental high, all of them together. It's almost like being possessed."

—*Joe Greene*

"The first couple of plays, I'm super aggressive. I'm out of my stance and on the guy. . . . I want to establish that he's going to get manhandled."

"You go for it. All the stops are out. Caution is to the wind, and you're battling with everything you have. That's the real fun of the game."

*—Dan Dierdorf*

"Confidence is the result of hours and days and weeks and years of constant work and dedication."

*—Roger Staubach*

"It's all right to relax off the field, but on Sunday everything has to be quick. . . . If you're too relaxed and lackadaisical, you sort of ease into things instead of jumping right on."

*—Joe Namath*

"As you get older, maybe you get a half step slower, so you try to do anything you can to make it up, to make good. Whatever the price, I'm willing to pay it."

"The world does owe us a living. The only thing is this: we have to go out and collect."

*—Don Maynard*

"I'm going to play every game I can, and I'm going to give it all I've got every time I play. When I get done I'm going to be able to say that I gave it hell while I was in it."

*—Floyd Little*

"The defenses are more sophisticated now, but I don't think they confuse me. They don't upset me. You just have to keep on learning every year. There's no secret. You have to apply yourself and work at it."

*—George Blanda*

"I just believe that whatever it is you can do, you should do the best you can. Put your all into it. If you don't utilize your talents, don't cultivate them, make them grow, then that's a shame. It's a sin, really."

*—Harry Carson*

"The thing I admired was that he demanded the very best—and then some. . . . It's exciting to be suddenly in a situation where you and everyone around you are trying their very best to do something well."

"I really think Lombardi considered loafing a worse sin than adultery. . . . This is the way he reasoned: show me a man who loafs and I'll show you a man who despises himself, and all his teammates."

*—Larry Brown*

"You have to keep doing things like that. You have to expand yourself physically, expand yourself mentally, do different things. Then it'll come."

—Dewey Selmon

"When you finally reach the solution it is very self-supporting. It confirms in your mind that you *can* do it, that if you try hard and keep chipping away, you'll get there. A proper solution validates all your effort."

—Frank Ryan

# Honest Assessment

"I think if a runner gets hurt it's his own fault. I've only been hurt once—a twisted knee—and that was my own carelessness."

"Don't blame anybody else for what comes down on you. Whatever happens, you *let* it happen. You deserve it. So don't give me any excuses."

"A man has to know his own abilities. He has to know what it takes to get the job done. He has to have been there and back, and know how he did it."

—O. J. Simpson

"We don't make any excuses. If a guy isn't playing well, you go up and tell him."

—O. J. Simpson
(quoting Lou Saban)

"The reasons his statement had such magnitude is that he had never said anything like that before in his six years with the team. He's not boastful. He's not a braggart. He just said it as a matter of fact. 'We *are* the best team.' "

"You have to be critical of yourself. Not supercritical, but you have to call the play as it is."

"When you have plans, you can get into your history. You can chronicle your progress and reflect back on what's happened. Did I do what I planned? . . . You have a measuring stick of how far you've come and how far there is to go. It keeps you growing."

"We review every game on film the following Tuesday, and that's how we check up on our effectiveness in sticking to our plan. If there are any mistakes, we find them. If we do it right, it feels very good to watch it."

—Joe Greene

"Pass blocking is like a precise dance step, and it has to be perfect time after time. . . . There is only one way I know to be sure that it is. You have to study yourself every day."

—Dan Dierdorf

"I just believe that the more critical you are of your own performance—the higher the standards you have—the better you become at what you do."

"I think you can learn about your problems faster if you have some help than if you try to find out everything on your own."

—Don Maynard

"He hardly said a word. . . . But the message gets across. You begin to think about yourself, how well you've been doing. You start to concentrate more without even trying."

"He's making sure of your self-awareness. He doesn't want you out there like a zombie. He wants you thinking, being alive to your situation."

—Russ Francis

"Embarrassment is a great motivator. There are some people who play very, very well just so they don't get embarrassed in front of their friends and a national audience."

—Lynn Swann

"I look around the league and I have to ask, Who hits like I do? My style is of such an aggressive nature that if I slack off sometimes I'm back to what everybody else is doing normally."

"I got a lot of recognition last year. I was all this and all that. But what does it really mean? . . . You have to be realistic. Basically, all I do is entertain people."

—Willie Lanier

"I found out I was trying to force myself that way. I was playing a mind game on myself. . . . What I found out was that it just wasn't *me*. It wasn't right for me. I had to completely reorganize myself."

"We need to know ourselves. We have to find what *we* are best suited for. . . . The game is to figure . . . out what is our *best* goal. Then we go for that. We master that."

—Dewey Selmon